REVIEWING
FOR THE
MASS MEDIA

REVIEWING FOR THE MASS MEDIA

Todd Hunt

CHILTON BOOK COMPANY

Philadelphia New York London

Copyright © 1972 by Todd Hunt
First Edition   All Rights Reserved
Published in Philadelphia by Chilton Book Company
and simultaneously in Ontario, Canada,
by Thomas Nelson & Sons, Ltd.
Designed by Cypher Associates
Manufactured in the United States of America

Library of Congress Cataloging in Publication Data

Hunt, Todd.
  Reviewing for the mass media.

  Bibliography: p. 177
  1. Newspapers—Sections, columns, etc.—Reviews.
I. Title.
PN4784.R4H8 PA P   070.4'42   72-5850
ISBN 0-8019-5733-8

Acknowledgments

Sincere thanks are extended to *The New York Times, Time* magazine and *Book World* for granting permission to reprint substantial excerpts from copyrighted reviews that first appeared in their pages. I am also indebted to the many writers and publications mentioned throughout from which I obtained short illustrations of method and form.

The following Rutgers University students prepared studies which provided material for this book: Laurence Anderson, Nancy Bevilacqua, Susan Ferris, Richard Hubbard and Paul Quijano.

Ernest Albrecht, drama critic for the *Home News* in New Brunswick, N. J., permitted the author to accompany him on numerous opening nights, on and off Broadway.

Barbara Duska typed the manuscript and associated materials.

A grant from the Rutgers College Research Council supported some of the research and preparation.

Contents

REVIEWING
FOR THE
MASS MEDIA

I
Who Cares
if the Critics
Like It?

The clerk in Higbee's book department waits patiently while the customer rummages through her purse in search of the clipping from the *Plain Dealer's* book page. "Oh, yes," she smiles. "That's the third request we've had for it today."

Outside the Morosco Theatre, secretaries and businessmen on their lunch hour queue up halfway to the corner of Broadway and 45th, hoping to get tickets any time, any location, any price to the musical comedy that this morning's *Times* called "the season's brightest!"

Beaming with approval over his breakfast coffee, the manager of Grauman's Chinese Theatre in Hollywood listens as Judith Crist tells the NBC *Today* audience of millions that the latest John Wayne epic is a "lusty, brawling, shoot-em-up like Hollywood used to make." That'll look good on the marquee.

The American book publishing industry is producing 2,000 new novels and 18,000 new nonfiction books a year. Filmmakers annually turn out almost 300 feature-length movies, and foreign imports double the total. The television networks introduce from thirty to forty new shows in a two-week period each autumn, and when they falter, a flood of "specials" and documentaries replaces them in the winter and spring. Fifty shows a year is Broadway's pace, but off-Broadway, regional, campus and strawhat theater give the national audience a much wider choice. Sculpture, painting, dance, music and all manner of cultural activity are thriving.

Blessed with this cornucopia of arts, entertainment and leisure-time activity, the American public seeks guidance and advice from its mass media. And, commensurate with the overwhelming number of choices, there is an overwhelming amount of guidance and advice. The critical review is one of the hallmarks of American journalism, and in recent years it has become not only a print phenomenon but a staple of broadcast journalism as well.

If we have typical reading and viewing habits, we come across half a dozen book, film and television reviews in our morning paper, we hear at least one film or play review from the broadcast media, and we are exposed to many more if we pick up a magazine. In recent years even *Life*, once a photo-essay vehicle, has altered its format to give prominent up-front display to film and book columns.

That publishers and producers believe reviews are important is obvious from the prominence they give to excerpts from favorable notices. Well-established renegades such as Broadway producer David Merrick and author Gore Vidal occasionally outmaneuver the media in order to present an artistic work to the public in a pristine, uncriticized state. But most of the nation's arts and entertainment entrepreneurs depend on the advance copy of a book, the special screening of a film, the previews and opening night ritual of the stage play to generate copy and commentary, whetting the public's appetite and building an audience.

At a March, 1970, press conference called to release the results of a nationwide Louis Harris and Associates pilot study of criticism in America, the Rev. Everett C. Parker, director of the sponsoring office of communications of the United Church of Christ, cited the indispensable role of criticism in modern society. "A key element in the quality of life in any society is the state of its criticism," he said. "If criticism of the mass media and the arts comes to no more than puffery and cheap praise, there is a danger of a public lulled into noncritical acceptance of the banal, the sentimental or the simply untrue."

Puffery and cheap praise. They were virtually synonymous with "notices" or reviews in the England of two centuries ago. It was not an uncommon practice then to bribe reviewers to ensure favorable endorsements in the newspapers and magazines. Today such blatant practices are rare. But book reviews in the mass media were deplored as "mere shopping guides" by a panelist during National Book Awards Week a few years ago.

Critics have been chastised and condemned through the years for supposedly deriving sadistic glee from their swift, systematic dismemberment and interment of works that may reflect an artist's life work. An occasional critic may have just such a blood lust, but like most extreme judgments it does not characterize the field.

The extremes of puffery and sadism aside, the great body of reviews, notices and criticism in the mass media can be characterized as an important *public service*. Before analyzing the craft in any detail, we should itemize the ways in which the aspiring reviewer will serve his public:

(1) Above all, the reviewer informs his readers.

We are talking about the "reviewer"—the journalistic writer whose primary obligation is to inform, to report, to take notice of what is new. He may be differentiated from the literary or artistic "critic" who writes for specialized journals or literary magazines, usually under less deadline pressure.

When a play opens on Broadway, when a book is published, when a new western comes to the local movie house, they are preceded by all the heralds of the entertainment industry: publicity, announcements, guest appearances, promotional stunts and advertisements. But the actualization of the event is dependent upon the critical review in the local newspaper. Publication of the review signals a change in the status of the work: it is now among us; it has herewith received its first judgment; it is henceforth a subject for serious discussion. Review copies of a book are distributed weeks in advance, a play "previews" for days or weeks, and a film's reputation begins to build when the first columnist appears on the set. But the public willingly accepts the dose of one percent silver nitrate and the spank on the bottom administered by the reviewer as the official moment of birth.

Indeed, the critical notice is often the be-all and end-all for many. "I never read novels," evangelist Billy Graham told an interviewer from *Cosmopolitan*. "I read *about* the novels in the reviews." He continued: "In my talks, I allude to more movies than I see, because here, too, I depend upon the reviews . . . I get much of my material from listening to Judith Crist on the *Today Show*."

(2) He raises the cultural level of the community.

"In the hinterlands," wrote music critic Ronald Eyer in *Opera News*, "the critic often as not finds his role to be that of teacher and civic leader in addition to reviewer. He often has to spell out the significance and importance of works that are familiar elsewhere, and he may even feel constrained to beat the drum for music he fears his public would slight."

Even in the most cosmopolitan city, education and audience-building are major concerns of dance, music and art critics. In a later chapter we will see that the predominant format or structure found in their reviews is the didactic lead segment, followed by an appraisal of how the artist under consideration served the work or the genre.

And even in cities where the arts are adequately subscribed and patronized, the critic finds himself involved with the cultural establishment's perpetual drive to ensure a prominent place for the arts. The late John K. Sherman of the Minneapolis *Star* and *Tribune*, dean of the Twin Cities area critics, was instrumental in preparing his community of two million Midwesterners to accept and support such rare blessings as the Tyrone Guthrie Theatre and the Walker Art Center. Augmenting his reviews with a weekly column and occasional reportorial pieces, he helped create a climate in which the arts could flourish.

Concludes Ronald Eyer: "Many critics agree that the work of the small-town critic can, if properly performed, be of more strategic and historic importance than that of his metropolitan colleague, since he is in a position to help mold public taste and create intelligent audiences where none existed before."

(3) He imparts personality to the community.

Closely related is the role the reviewer plays in building civic pride and identity, fostering an awareness of the special character of his city and its own particular cultural milieu.

In the mid-1960s, a brash young man named John Huddy moved from the police beat of the Columbus, Ohio, *Dispatch* to the movie review column after convincing the editors that he could best assay the films aimed at the growing youth audience.

Within a matter of months he was also covering all live entertainment in a thrice-weekly column called "My Kind of Town." He attacked the city's drab self-image with an effervescent, prideful style. Why did night club performers bring their pre-New York tryouts to Columbus? Because of the sophisticated, appreciative audiences. Why attend the new topical review? Because it is slick, witty and available only in America's leading cities.

Amazingly, the élan was contagious. People had grown so accustomed to saying and believing Columbus was the country's largest small town that it became so. Huddy gave them reason to expect better. His talent and enthusiasm quickly brought him a bid to make Miami his kind of town and the *Herald*'s entertainment editorship his kind of job.

(4) He advises readers how best to use their resources.

The panelist who termed review pages "mere shopping guides" may have been justified in questioning the quality of criticism. But to denigrate reviewers for helping the public spend limited time and money wisely is to ignore an important function of the mass media.

There are places in the world where grand opera of the highest caliber can be seen for 500 lire (80 cents), and there are university towns in this country where the Cleveland Orchestra plays a one-night stand in the gymnasium. In these places, the individual needs little help with his decision.

But where there are many events to choose from—worthy films, drama, dance and music events—and the prices range from $3 to $15, the reviewer is abandoning his responsibility if he fails to steer the public toward the uncommon, the innovative, the excellent.

(5) He helps artists and performers.

Henry James wrote in his essay *Criticism* that "one sees the critic as the real helper of the artist, a torch-bearing outrider, the interpreter, the brother."

Beyond furnishing the artist or performer with a scrapbook brimming with favorable notices, the writer of reviews provides valuable services. Unlike friends, associates and politely appreciative audiences, the reviewer takes a singular stance: What can I observe and reveal that will help this artist reach and enlighten the audience with which he is striving to communicate?

In a talk to Rutgers University students, drama critic Clive Barnes of *The New York Times* lamented that he and his colleagues were not sufficiently able to act as a "bridge" between audience and performer. His words echoed those of playwright Edward Albee, who told members of a theater workshop in Waterford, Connecticut: "A conscientious critic who loves the theater must try to help the writer and the audience meet each other half way. That bridge must not be bombed."

The critic is a member of the audience. But his loyalties are evenly divided. He is as much the agent of the artist, planted out front to detect what is right and what is wrong. His review is an intelligence report that can be used to considerable advantage.

(6) He defines the new.

Clad only in breechcloths, the writhing actors chant nonsense words and stick their tongues out at no one in particular. Then they urge the audience to follow them out of the theater and into the street. What is it?

"A new form," explains Alain Robbe-Grillet, "always seems to be more or less an absence of any form at all, since it is unconsciously judged by reference to consecrated forms."

Like science, the arts are developing at an accelerating rate. In another century, a French Academy might enforce painting standards and preserve order. In the 1970s, the Op and Pop of the previous decade are old stuff. Confronted with previously unimaginable works, the critic must be able to discern continuity, assess worth, bring meaning to apparent chaos. Or if it be sham, he must be able to recognize and debunk it. This challenge is perhaps his greatest.

(7) He records an important segment of history.

Every journalist is a servant of the historian. Doubtless, that is one reason editors demand so-called "objectivity" in their reporters' accounts. Facts must be laid down with unfailing accuracy so that later generations might correctly analyze the importance of our time.

Reviews published on a regular basis in the arts and entertainment sections of the nation's newspapers and magazines provide a record of what our artists have attempted to tell us and how we responded to their messages.

It is valuable, for example, to observe that a dozen plays in the

1970–71 off-Broadway season used nudity to deal explicitly with sexual themes, that they appealed to limited audiences rather than to the generally curious throngs which were drawn to *Hair* and *Oh! Calcutta!*, that they were generally inept and inane pieces of playwrighting, and that many lasted only a few nights after opening.

It will be interesting, too, for historians to catalog and analyze the artistic output of the 1960s, as documented in thousands of reviews, for insight into American artists' and the public's response to events in Southeast Asia. There will, of course, be the scathing *Macbird*, which laid the blame for John Kennedy's assassination and our subsequent involvement in Vietnam at Lyndon Johnson's feet in no uncertain terms. There will be a few other off-Broadway plays: *Summertree, Pinkville, The Trial of the Catonsville Nine.* And there will be *Joe*, a film which mirrored the frustrations and alienation of Americans in different walks of life. But perhaps the most telling information yielded by the data will concern the inability or unwillingness of artists and audiences alike to deal with the root issues, culminating in an escapist rush toward "nostalgia" as the disquieting decade drew to a close.

A play may last but a night or a season. The life of a film, prolonged perhaps by television exposure, is also limited. Art, music and dance are eternal, but performances are only brief moments. Critical reviews, however, are microfilmed and cataloged. No doubt some of them are even encapsuled in the granite cornerstones of city halls and public libraries around the country, waiting for the scholars of 2001 and after.

(8) Not least of all, he entertains.

"Did you see what John Simon said about the new Shelley Winters one-acters? Listen: 'These plays are so boring that they make not only theatergoing, but, more perniciously, sex itself look like a waste of time.' Wow!"

Reviews draw gasps. They get laughs. And they are quoted. They are a form of entertainment in themselves, especially when they flow from the pen of a waspish dilettante or from the lips of a puckish commentator. People who haven't been to a movie for years perk up when Gene Shalit does his minute waltz on WNBC. Moustache twitching and eyes dancing mischievously, he skewers a pretentious film with his lightning tongue, chews it to bits with a few dry *bon mots*, and spits it out as undigestible. The boys in the studio crack up, and the viewer gets a good laugh along with the dose of opinion. Johnny Carson, who in New York comes on minutes later with his monologue, ought to pay Shalit a generous fee for being his warm-up man.

To be sure, purists (and artists) despair of the grandstanding that is part of reviewing. A critic ought to keep himself out of his analysis, they argue. And he certainly ought not to substitute his own "performance" for the one he means to criticize. The issue is central to any discussion of the critic's role, and it will be the subject of a later chapter.

Meanwhile, suffice it to say that many of our most famous critics through the years obviously considered themselves "on stage." George Bernard Shaw, H. L. Mencken, and to some extent the preeminent George Jean Nathan did many a turn and took many a bow in the course of criticizing the works of others.

A review can hardly be "objective." Its subjective nature encourages the writer to introduce himself, get involved, and ultimately entertain—even amuse or horrify—in his own right. His editor and his readers encourage him in this conceit by giving him their attention. Because of the nature of the mass media, with hundreds of interesting, exciting and involving items begging for our attention each day, the reviewer feels pressed to be something of a showman along with all the other things he does so well.

These are some of the ways a reviewer serves his public. Not every review fulfills all purposes, but each attempts to offer a combination of services.

Clive Barnes, probably the most influential critic in America, considering his position with the nation's leading newspaper in the country's entertainment capital, argues that he and his colleagues should be "informed enthusiasts," stimulating thought, provoking ideas, and propagating a critical attitude.

Critics sharpen our sensibilities. If they appear to be a caustic and negative lot, perhaps it is because the promoters of entertainment and the arts are overly enthusiastic. The advertisement that promises "an epic film" and the critic who labels it "pure trash" serve to define the outer limits. It is still up to the individual member of the audience to make his choice.

2
Life in
Culture Gulch

The media men who cover fires, murders, heat waves, political conventions and other such disasters usually have a disdainful appellation for critics and reviewers. On larger newspapers, the arts desk may be called Culture Gulch. And the lone reviewer for a broadcast station or a small paper is the Culture Vulture. These are not very clever names; the reviewer's smug sense of superiority need hardly be rattled by such childish monickers.

Before examining the individual critic or reviewer in detail, we should pay an introductory visit to Culture Gulch and get the lay of the land.

Let's look first at a medium-sized daily newspaper, circulation 70,000, in a Midwestern manufacturing town where a branch of the state university is situated. The arts and entertainment coverage is insufficient to warrant a full-time editor. One full page in the typical 36- to 64- page paper is tabbed "Entertainment Scene" and carries movie theater advertisements, the television listings, other related advertising, one review or locally produced feature article, and one wire service or syndicated feature, plus a "Movie Timetable" boxed item and various fillers.

In addition, one of the four sections of the 80-page Sunday paper (circulation 90,000) is tabbed "Family - Fun - Features." It includes a movie page, two partial pages of book reviews, a television page plus a pullout TV Week schedule. A four-color feature spot leads the section, and up to four partial pages are available for entertainment or cultural news. The same section includes women's news, society, hobbies, various columns and a teen page.

Assignments and contributions are handled by the city desk. An assistant city editor usually develops and assigns local stories, getting most of his tips from mailed-in "handouts" or news releases. All copy is processed by the universal copy desk. A copy reader with a professed interest in arts and entertainment spends approximately two hours each afternoon editing and laying out the page. (In his absence another copyreader may "throw the page together" in as little as half an hour—the format lends itself to a quick "clip and dummy" treatment.)

Now let's look at how the various review materials are prepared, and by whom.

DRAMA

The newspaper's drama critic is an assistant professor of English literature who teaches courses in Shakespeare and composition at the university. He's in his mid thirties, and he has been writing criticism since his undergraduate days. A speech and theater arts major, he wrote reviews first for the campus paper, later for daily papers in the college towns where he did his graduate work. His wife, who combined theater and fine arts in college, is a scene designer and has worked on campus and community productions through the years.

He is paid $25 for each review, and he writes about 70 reviews each year. In addition to the university theater—which mounts a four-play "season" plus half a dozen lesser productions in-the-round—he reviews an off-campus "town-and-gown" coffeehouse, occasional productions by two religious foundation groups, and the six-play theater-in-barn summer season in an adjoining town. Along with the two or three dramatic productions included in the university's concerts and lectures program, the local reviewing amounts to about 35 plays annually.

Just 75 miles away—little over an hour by freeway—the center city has two legitimate theaters, one used by a resident company and the other bringing in a dozen road companies or pre-Broadway tryouts each year, seven of them on a subscription series. Most of the plays run one or two weeks and attract theatergoers from a regional area that includes parts of two states, a population of more than a million. The drama man makes it his practice to review opening nights of all productions in the center city.

The remainder of his output comes as a result of an annual pilgrimage to Broadway. He usually makes the trip late in November, after a dozen or more plays have begun their runs and before the holidays begin to attract people from his area to New York for shopping and theatergoing. For his New York reviews he is paid the usual $25, plus $100 for expenses during the four-day visit.

Finally, he writes a weekly "Spotlight" column for the Sunday entertainment section, usually focusing on behind-the-scenes information about local productions but occasionally offering opinions and ideas about the theater in general. The Sunday column also pays the flat $25. His income from reviewing, all told, amounts to about $2,000.

The drama man turns his material in to the city desk—almost always 120 lines of copy, which comes to 30 column inches. If any changes other than punctuation or spelling are made in his copy, he is usually called at home or the office. The system works to everyone's satisfaction, and there has been no recurrence of the unpleasantness created when his predecessor became part of the off-campus coffeehouse's "avant-garde clique" and permitted the association to seriously bias his judgments.

Music

The music reviewing situation is not quite so placid. Until recently, all orchestral and ballet events, both on the campus and in the center city, were regularly reviewed by a venerable woman nearing 60, the wife of a prominent local physician, herself both an accomplished musician and a former piano teacher. She was the paper's first reviewer, contributing reports for the prestige of the by-line as early as the 1930s, and earning considerable local fame when certain of her essays were printed by the popular *Etude* magazine. Her writing is flowery, and she affects such phrases as "this writer" and "to the music *cognoscenti*" while imposing her own tastes and standards on the reader and the music world. But she is something of a local institution, and the editors have never been able to bring themselves to suggest that she step down.

Instead, responding to pressures from a few perennial letter-writers and critics of the critic, the editors jumped at the offer of a young woman, working in the newspaper's circulation department and attending college part time, who asked to write reviews of popular musical events. She proved to be not only quite knowledgeable about all types of music but even in possession of a crisp, lively style of writing. It's no secret in the newsroom that she'll take over all music reviewing assignments eventually. Some friction has resulted—when musical events fall in the gray zone between popular and classical, the Queen Bee frequently displays fickle temperament in deciding what she will cover and what she'll leave to the neophyte. On at least one occasion, the managing editor has had to referee a dispute.

Books

The assistant Sunday editor is, by job definition, in charge of the book-reviewing setup, although it is no secret that his superiors, the Sunday editor and the managing editor, exercise the prerogative of reviewing major books destined for the best-seller list. The Sunday editor takes many of the name-author novels, and the managing editor lays first claim to political books.

When cartons of review books come in, a secretary types a card for each. Then the book editor scans the books and stack of cards, noting how many words he wants for each—perhaps 500 words on a major work, but frequently no more than a 50-word blurb on run-of-the-mill items. The secretary posts a weekly list of review books on the bulletin board in the newsroom, and reporters and editors quickly sign up for the titles that interest them. Reviews are due in two weeks. There is no payment, but the reviewer keeps the book. There is occasional grumbling that senior editors always seem to get the $25 art books while general assignment reporters are left with mysteries and paperback reprints.

While the system seems to be a first-come, first-served free-for-all, the assistant Sunday editor tries to channel certain special interest titles to staff members with expertise on the topic. One copy editor, for example, is a science buff. The sports editor gets the books by or about athletes. In addition, professors at the university are occasionally asked to review highly technical or specialized books.

The system, while lax at times, produces about two dozen reviews each week. Most are competent and interesting enough to serve the needs of the typical reader, and occasionally a review from the paper is quoted on a second-edition dust jacket.

FILMS

This is the area of current dispute. Old-timers in green eyeshades remember the days when a daily column on the entertainment page "reviewed" local movies. It was written by the advertising department and shamelessly puffed the latest double bill to come off the Hollywood production line. The column was dropped in postwar years, when movie attendance declined and all but two downtown theaters, plus a campus "classic" house and an "art" theater featuring stag films, were closed or turned into supermarkets.

When films began to be treated as a serious art form in the 1960s, the paper was approached by various staff members and outside writers concerning regular movie reviews. The drama critic added fuel when he reviewed film adaptations of *Marat/Sade* and *Romeo and Juliet* on the premise that it was interesting and important to compare and contrast stage presentations with versions in a second medium.

Why, then, is there no regular film critic? Ask any editor or staff member and you get a different explanation. Inertia ("We've never done it that way") is, of course, a fact of life in newspapering. Another explanation is that the paper already pays for reams of Hollywood copy in the form of syndicated material and wire service features. (It comes with a choice of glossies several weeks before the movie arrives in town, so it can be easily set in type and run at any time.) A cynical observation is that the two downtown houses are owned by a big local businessman who has on occasion mentioned to the publisher over a scotch and water at the country club that "our ads and the timetable tell the audience all they need to know, and, besides, who in this town is competent to criticize a multimillion-dollar picture?"

Shameful as the lack of movie reviews may be to film buffs, one can at least argue that in the meantime the need for critical notice is fulfilled by a myriad of national magazines. The lack of a local film critic is not as serious as a vacancy in the drama or the music post would be.

TELEVISION

The newspaper belongs to the Associated Press and uses the daily television column provided by the wire service.

The preceding is a composite view, one that would be recognized by almost any newsman on a newspaper of similar size and situation. Of course there are a dozen or so major cities in the country where the resources of the newspaper and the abundant cultural life create a situation in which criticism of greater breadth and higher caliber can flourish. In these few situations, the $25-an-item reviewer and the piecemeal book review section give way to full-time cultural news operations.

ALL THE CULTURAL NEWS THAT IS FIT TO PRINT

Leading the field, of course, is the nation's most influential paper, *The New York Times*. The mammoth Sunday edition is the nearest thing we have in this country to a national newspaper. Emanating from the nation's leading center of book publishing, play production, art, dance, opera and television programming, it carries word of developments in all these fields to far-flung readers who pay as much as a dollar a copy.

Times book reviews alone exceed the amount of coverage given all of the arts in most other papers. The typical 84-page daily edition devotes an entire page to advertisements for books. Editorial matter includes, besides the crossword puzzle and a bridge column, one or two book reviews of from 750 to 1,000 words in length, and a list of books published that day by U. S. publishers. Three regular reviewers handle most of the novels and nonfiction, with other staff members or assigned reviewers handling specialized books.

The tab-sized 24- to 60-page book review Sunday supplement is a separate entity; in effect it is a magazine about books and the book world. Many books reviewed by the daily staff are independently assigned by the Sunday editors to outside reviewers, frequently with results that vary greatly. It is possible for a book to get a rave on Tuesday and a pan on Sunday, a situation which former *Times* editor Turner Catledge called "counterbalancing our critics' impact" in order to avoid the complaint that the paper has the power to dictate success or failure in cultural endeavors.

Nearly two dozen persons are employed by the *Times* Book Review. Approximately a third of the 7,500 books received each year are given some sort of review, often only a few paragraphs in one of the several departments for short takes: Reader's Report, Et Al, For Young Readers, Criminals at Large. Fifteen or twenty books each week get full reviews, sometimes in groups of two or three related titles, other times with accompanying essays concerning a special aspect of the book or its author.

Review copies are first screened by editors who must decide whether the book is worth a review, what "play" or prominence the review should receive, and ultimately who should be invited to do the review. Contributors frequently include authors who have written on the same subject, as well as college professors, critics from other media, specialists on the *Times* staff, and occasionally even an elected official or a personality from the entertainment world. The mayor of New York, for example, may review a book on urban problems, and his book, in turn, will be reviewed by a noted professor of political science.

The *Times'* book review section is preeminent in the field; its analysis based on reports from 125 bookstores in 64 U. S. communities, for example, is generally accepted as *the* best-seller list to which authors aspire. A few magazines aimed at intellectuals, such as the *New York Review of Books*, carry as many reviews. But only two other media reach as large and democratic an audience—the similar but smaller *Book World* supplement distributed jointly by the *Washington Post* and the *Chicago Tribune* on Sundays, and the 600,000-circulation *Saturday Review* weekly magazine.

The cultural staff of the daily *Times* numbers approximately 40 regular employees, augmented by numerous stringers such as the dozen or more music reviewers whose six-inch notices concerning weekend chamber music concerts around the city are clustered together in Monday morning's edition. In every major area—drama, dance, films, music and art—there is depth. Two or three simultaneous openings needn't daunt the top critic.

In 1962, in an effort to relate reviews and criticism to the "cultural explosion" sweeping the country, the paper's arts and entertainment staff was flushed from its cubbyhole behind the west wall and reunited with the news staff—literally and figuratively. But Culture Gulch still manages to be a less hectic place than the rest of the third floor newsroom. The assistant editor for cultural news is the focal point of the department. He coordinates the activities of the individual units; for example, the three film critics may huddle in the early afternoon to divide up review assignments for the next few days, and then they'll check with the assistant editor, giving him the schedule and receiving an indication of how much space is available for each review.

Later in the afternoon, as the writers complete their reviews, a neat stack of copy grows on the assistant editor's desk. He reads through it all, checking for oversights and for proper newspaper style, then sends it on to the composing room. Compared with the sometimes frenzied activity in the "bullpen" where regular news is processed, Culture Gulch is quiet. The reviewers "write to space," and their copy requires only an occasional conference or questioning.

Late reviews, such as of a Broadway opening or the opera, require a make-over for the final edition. A prescribed number of lines is assigned to the critic, who turns the copy out on deadline.

As in every other area, the *Times* is able to give culture superb saturation coverage should the occasion warrant it. When the new $46-million Metropolitan Opera House at Lincoln Center opened in 1966, the paper sent not only its music critic to review the premier production but also the ballet critic to assay the dancing, the art critic to evaluate the decor, the architecture critic to "review" the building itself, and the top society writer to sum up the audience. (There wasn't a rave review in the lot; even the people were described as a "mob" of "overachievers.")

Small paper or large, and in broadcasting too, cultural affairs is an area of increasing importance. In the next chapter we will take a closer look at the individuals who make their home in Culture Gulch.

3
Where Does
He Get Off?

When a halfback drops two successive touchdown passes in the end zone, the sportswriters report that he "had a bad day."

A reviewer, to judge from the letters to the editor that follow in the wake of a negative review, doesn't get the benefit of the doubt. The correspondents assume that the critic is born mean, bred to kill, bound and determined to do evil. Here's just a sampling of what to expect:

When a college English professor wrote in *Saturday Review* that a collection of short stories by National Book Award winner Joyce Carol Oates failed to achieve "greatness," she fired off a letter to the editor demanding to know "Where are the 'great' reviewers of our day? Frankly, I have never heard of [the reviewer]." Her tone reflected the "Where does he get the right to say those things?" attitude prevalent in many such letters.

Interviewed after the majority of critics had rejected his play *All Over*, playwright Edward Albee was quoted as saying: "The majority of our critics are best qualified to cover brush fires in New Jersey." He went right down the list of his antagonists. For example: "There is no excuse for John Simon, except his own need to create a John Simon."

British filmmaker David Lean, quoted by the Associated Press regarding the critics' unfavorable reaction to *Lawrence of Arabia* and *Doctor Zhivago*, had this explanation: "They all want my job."

Composer Igor Stravinsky, shortly before his death, snapped back at Clive Barnes for his pan of a production of *The Firebird*. He raised questions about Barnes's job: "Why does Mr. Barnes call me a 'querulous old man' when he has so plainly picked the 'querul' himself? Is it because of the growing complaints about his facile reviews and the way they oscillate between the 'rave' for one kind of mediocrity and the 'roast' for another kind?"

In his lecture on Shakespeare and Milton, Samuel Taylor Coleridge said, "Reviewers are usually people who would have been poets, historians, biographers, if they could; they have tried their talents at one or the other, and have failed; therefore they turn critics."

Who *are* the critics? How do they get started? What are their qualifications?

Many writers in the field of arts and entertainment are, indeed, people who have been poets, historians and biographers. But they have not necessarily failed. Coming over to the critical calling doesn't indicate a lack of talent or creativity. Most of the successful ones consider their background in the arts to be *training* for the eventual avocation. Indeed, a reviewer who has enriched his background by first participating in the cultural world as a writer or an artist may in many ways be better prepared to understand a work and to judge it than the reviewer who springs full blown as a critic. Edgar Allan Poe and George Bernard Shaw are two who crossed the line so many times that they are remembered equally for their criticism and for their artistic output.

START ANYWHERE, BUT START EARLY

Pulitzer Prize-winning music critic Harold Schonberg began piano lessons at the age of three, and he decided at twelve to become a critic because of his love for music and an early realization that "you can get paid for listening to music." He started writing while in college, and he soon had a monthly column in *Musical Advance*. After earning a Master of Arts degree in music and English, he worked for *American Music Lover* magazine. Following military service in World War Two, he was a music critic first at the *New York Sun* and later for *The New York Times*. Along the way he wrote several books about musicians, composers and conductors.

Dwight Macdonald, a staff writer for *Fortune* and *The New Yorker* before becoming movie critic and later political columnist for *Esquire,* is another example of an early bloomer. A bookworm at Barnard School for Boys and later at Phillips Exeter Academy, he was encouraged by his teachers to try writing. He founded a literary club and helped edit the school literary magazine. At Yale, too, he was an editor of the literary magazine. After a start as an executive trainee at Macy's (more out of necessity than desire) he entered the magazine business. In the 1930s he helped revive *Partisan Review.* In addition to his articles for magazines, he is a frequent contributor to book review supplements, and he has published a collection of his critical essays on film during the 1960s.

Rex Reed was campus critic and editor of the literary magazine at Louisiana State University. Turned down by *The New York Times* for a writing job (they offered him a position as a copy boy) he bided his time in a succession of jobs. In 1965 he attended the Venice Film Festival on his own and submitted interviews with Jean-Paul Belmondo and Buster Keaton to the *Times* and the *New York Herald-Tribune,* respectively. That was the breakthrough, and now his articles and movie reviews appear in numerous periodicals, he is a frequent talk-show guest, and two collections of his interviews have sold well in hardcover books.

Pauline Kael majored in philosophy at the University of California at Berkeley, worked at a bookstore and a publishing house, and even did seamstress work at home. All the while she pursued her interest in the movies, and in writing. Eventually her broadcasts on movies for a Berkeley radio station led to a job managing an art movie house. Reprints of her radio reviews in *Film Quarterly* brought her to the attention of the Eastern press, and she came to New York to write about films for *Life,* then *Atlantic, Vogue, McCalls, The New Republic* and finally *The New Yorker.* Unlike some of the stars she writes about or the heroes of the movies she reviews, she didn't fight and claw her way to the top. (She doesn't even use a typewriter.) Her passion for films, her capacity for thorough research, and her straightforward, unflashy writing have carried her to a position as the country's most respected film critic.

Longtime *New York Times* drama critic Brooks Atkinson taught

English at Dartmouth and covered the police beat for the Boston *Transcript*. He began writing reviews on his own time under the tutelage of the *Transcript*'s regular critic. He became critic for the *Times* just eight years after graduating from Harvard. An equally short path was followed by Renata Adler: Bryn Mawr, the Sorbonne, a master's degree in comparative literature at Harvard, five years on the staff of *The New Yorker*, and then into the *Times* film review slot.

George Jean Nathan, probably this country's greatest critic, never knew another life; in a remarkable half-century-long career he served as critic at various times for more than a dozen magazines and two major papers. He wrote some 30 books, edited the *Theatre Book of the Year* from 1943 to 1951, and contributed articles on the arts to *Encyclopedia Britannica*.

Stanley Kauffmann, film critic of *The New Republic*, trained for the theater in college, wrote plays and novels, directed summer theater, and spent ten years in repertory companies before he joined the magazine. He has also served briefly as drama critic for WNET public television in New York and for the *Times*.

WHAT KIND OF BACKGROUND?

Most critics are college educated. The university years provide an opportunity to become acquainted with the arts, and also an opportunity to write about them in the campus media. But the lack of a degree need not preclude a career in criticism, as the television reviewer for one of country's leading papers can attest. Knowledge of the field, critical ability and writing talent are considerably more important than formal education.

A better argument could be started over whether or not mass media writing experience is necessary in order to write for the large audience. Atkinson, Wolcott Gibbs and others were top-notch reporters first. But there are many who would argue that the pressures of the newsroom breed sloppiness, not quality essays. Most English departments disdain work in the mass media and steer their brighter students toward contributing to reviews, anthologies and highbrow campus media untainted by journalistic conventions of style and format. In the end, the argument appears almost unresolvable, for successful critics have taken every route conceivable.

Even though one is trained for basic newspaper reporting (the sentence has been purposely constructed to avoid the words "profession" and "art," both of which can lead to further arguments), how does one escape the obit desk and win the reviewer's mantle?

Start by indicating an interest in culture, the arts and reviews the day you are hired. The managing editor usually extends the courtesy of a short "What do you hope to do?" interview before consigning a neophyte to the rewrite man. Keep the managing editor reminded thereafter, as well as the news editor and the city editor—anyone who assigns stories. Let them know you'd like to write news stories and feature pieces in the broad arts and entertainment area. An assignment may lead to a contact and eventually to a review, perhaps in a field not previously handled by the paper's established reviewers.

The book review department is a good place to begin looking for tasks, even if it only means 50-word reviews of humor anthologies and books of animal stories that rate nothing more than initials at the end. In addition, hand in an occasional unsolicited review—live folk music performances at a local church-sponsored teen club may be worthy of coverage although they haven't come to the attention of the editors or the senior reviewer. The worst the editors can do is spindle your piece. More likely, they'll find space for it. Another thing to keep in mind is that there is a wealth of popular summer entertainment in barns and public parks, under tents and at local fairs and festivals. It comes around just when the regular reviewers are taking their vacations. Many newspapers spread complimentary or review tickets for summer events around among the younger staffers. It's a perfect opportunity to show that you can handle the job.

What "authority" is necessary?

Now to the most awesome question facing the young reviewer: What authority do I have to judge a work, and how should I exercise it?

That, of course, is no simple matter. It is, in essence, the underlying issue whenever the performance of a critic is called into question by a producer, an artist, an irate member of the audience, or sometimes even the editor. Before setting a single word of praise or admonition down on paper, the reviewer should become well acquainted with the arguments regarding his rights and responsibilities.

Two concepts should dominate any discussion:

(1) The reviewer must have a profound concern for the perpetuation and improvement of the art form to which he addresses himself; that concern should transcend his own ego as well as the sensibilities of any other individuals.

(2) The reviewer must remember that he is basically a newsman, covering newsworthy events for the benefit of a mass audience, an important task that is in no way diminished merely because he also has the privilege of offering subjective evaluation.

Judith Crist unabashedly admits that she "loves" movies: "Why bother to criticize if you don't care?" Only the person who cares can demand an adherence to a standard, can dream of the possible perfection, can recognize integrity on the one hand and a lack of it on the other, she has stated.

A reviewer should really want, selfishly, to see and hear the best whenever he goes to the theater or the gallery. If he has high standards and high expectations, and if he can persuade others on both sides of the footlights to pursue them likewise, the "selfishness" will be beneficial to all.

If he has the necessary concern, it follows that he has much of the necessary preparation for reviewing, since one grows out of the other. The more he learns—through formal education, personal background, involvement and experience—the more his concern grows, and he is led in turn to do more research, become more committed. This personal, lifelong involvement is precisely why no career in criticism is quite like another and why no university can chart a guaranteed path leading to certification as an arbiter of culture.

The critical review is, generally speaking, an essay, and the essay form leads easily to authoritative, high-sounding statements and conclusions. Therein lies the usual cause of scorn for critics, the cries of "Says who?", unless the writer realizes that one man's reality is not another man's reality and makes an attempt to compensate.

DEALING WITH THE POWER

When Clive Barnes took over the *Times* drama desk, he found the "omnipotence" that comes with the job not to his liking. He set about to diminish his own undesired power in two ways. He abandoned the essay style somewhat and inserted an "I" wherever his opinions or concepts were personal rather than generally accepted. His pieces read more like conversations than those of his predecessors. More important, they sound less like judgments handed down from the Supreme Court of the Theater.

And, as Gay Talese noted in *The Kingdom and the Power*, Barnes developed a knack for "adroitly conveying two things at once, of sometimes both praising and criticizing a production in a single sentence." Although Talese's words were written two years earlier, they anticipated the following lead from a review of 1970's last musical:

Oh, dear! I come to bury *Lovely Ladies, Kind Gentlemen*, not to praise it, but there were one or two decent things, and three or four half-decent things, about this strangely dated musical that modestly opened Monday night at the Majestic Theater.

Here Barnes sacrifices syntax in favor of playing one element against another. Not only is it a poor sentence; it aroused the wrath of all Broadway. The phrase "I come to bury . . ." overshadowed everything else, and the whole issue of the power of the *Times* critic was fueled anew.

He was more adroit in his subsequent review of 1971's first musical:

No novel that has sold 20 million copies can be said to be devoid of popular interest, and although I have never read Leon Uris's novel *Exodus*, or even seen the film from it, it was clearly within its own terms of reference highly successful.

The musical *Ari*, which Mr. Uris has developed from his novel, just as clearly is not. It opened last night at the Mark Hellinger Theater, and can be praised more easily for its aspiration than its achievements.

Here Barnes has said it safely. He gives away one half of a debating point by noting the source material's popularity. When, after a lead paragraph that marks time, he brings himself to pan the show, he constructs a sentence that seems to say, diplomatically, "I disagree with you, but I'll defend your right to . . . etc."

Other critics concur in the voluntary diminution of unasked-for power. Richard Schickel, who reviews movies for *Life*, suggested: "The first obligation of the critic is to make his own position clear. But he should do so, I think, in a reasonable tone of voice and with a sense of his own limits and prejudices and blind spots."

What gets a reviewer into trouble, more often than not, is the notion that the critical piece must always be witty and bright. Toss off a *bon mot* here, a devilish pun there, and the subject matter be damned as long as the review is crisp, clever and memorable. Fortunately, good critics don't believe that anymore, just as reporters don't cover crime and punishment the way they did in the Twenties and Thirties, and sports columnists don't indulge in endless clichés, nicknames and other cute tricks of yesteryear.

"Jones played Beethoven last night, and Beethoven lost," they used to write. And in a later era, *Time* magazine was the prime culprit, displaying a breezy style that made word-coining a substitute for analysis: "cinemoppet" for child, and the like. Sometimes titles of forgettable flops cry out for the obvious lampoon: "*Score . . .* doesn't." "I say 'not never' to *Not Now, Darling.*" "Would that *Four on a Garden* were only *Two on a Garden.*" Such quotable quips are hard to pass up, and they do little damage. But when a reviewer mistakenly assumes that the proper way to write his piece is to line up one wisecrack after another, glorying in his own cleverness, nobody is served well.

THE READY-MADE REPUTATION

The reviewer does not need to devote much, if any, space to convincing his readers that he knows what he is talking about. Surveys show that the reputation of the medium attaches to its critics: a good newspaper is assumed to have qualified critics. At any rate, long paragraphs of credentials are needless, since an indication of the writer's competence comes across in the course of providing the readers with the background for the work under consideration. Although we will see in later chapters the need for "teaching" or preparing the reader in some types of reviews, especially dance, art and music, it does not mean "convincing him I know what I'm talking about." This is one of the hardest lessons for inexperienced or insecure reviewers to learn.

The second major contention—that the reviewer is first and foremost a *news* reporter—is one that should bring reassurance to the beginning reviewer. The first task facing a reviewer is to *describe* the work, a job not unlike the regular newsman's description of what happened at city council or in court. The reviewer's compression of a story into a four- or five-paragraph synopsis parallels the reporter's condensation of a complex issue into terse summary. The

24

reviewer is, of course, preoccupied with selecting appropriate adjectives and adverbs, but no less so than is the best journalist. One major difference in approach is that the reporter writes in an "inverted pyramid" format of ordering information from most important to least, while the reviewer may recount the plot chronologically, then turn to various aspects of the work one at a time, leading up to a final summary.

When all the requirements of newsworthiness and fidelity to the art form have been met, the reviewer's product stands squarely upon personal judgment. Confidence in one's ability to write reviews, therefore, is merely an extension of confidence in one's own judgment. The former book review editor of *Commentary* magazine summarized his standards of judgment this way: "Is the book of first-rate quality? Is it relevant to the questions and issues of our time?" Obviously he had his own concept of what "first-rate" means and what issues are relevant to our time. Similarly, Dwight Macdonald, while reviewing movies for *Esquire* magazine, had two criteria when evaluating a film: Did it change the way you looked at things? Did it stand the test of time?

"The critic," said B. H. Haggin, "writes not what is true, but what is true for him." As long as he represents his work accordingly, the intelligent reader will go along with him in the hope of increasing his own understanding and formulating his own value system.

4

Authoritarian
or Impressionist?

Closely related to the subject of a reviewer's "credentials" is the matter of his "philosophy," his theoretical concept of criticism. Perhaps the words "approach" or "attitude" better express it, since theory and philosophy can become too rigidly defined. In practice, few reviewers for the mass media espouse any particular school of criticism. It is academic people, for academic purposes, who give us these two polarities to contemplate: *authoritative* criticism versus *impressionistic*.

The authoritarian approach is highly comparative. The particular artistic work is evaluated in reference to historic models which have previously been judged worthy. The authoritarian critic must have considerable background preparation and exposure to the art form, and he necessarily accepts a set of fixed standards or rules.

Conversely, the impressionistic approach generates an expression of the critic's (or the audience's) reaction to the work, exclusive of standards or precedents. The work is judged on its own merits, in a singular context.

The impressionistic philosophy came to the fore in the 1920s and eventually came to be known as the "New Criticism." Its proponents argued against the strictures of "biographical" criticism, which judges the literary work in light of the author's previous endeavors, his personality, his milieu—in short, every possible "input" of information. Understandably, the theory was supported by a great number of poets and novelists. Most writers believe their works should speak for themselves.

Arguing for the impressionistic point of view in the early 1920s, Stuart Pratt Sherman summarized: "The object gives the standard. Confronted with heirlooms or with innovations, one's first question is: does this, or does it not, tend to assist the entire body of the people toward the best human life of which they are capable?"

But the authoritarian philosophy has predominated throughout history, dating perhaps from as early as 330 B. C., when Aristotle systemized the form and function of tragic drama in his *Poetics*. For centuries, church and crown dictated and enforced standards of artistic endeavor. Eighteenth-century British and nineteenth-century American essayists offered formulas for poetry, novels and criticism. The academies of art compelled painters and sculptors to assimilate the methods and skills of their predecessors, perpetuating the styles demanded by the patron.

To this day, several factors support the authoritarian: the formalized teaching of literature and the arts in the school systems, the need to win and consolidate public support, and the influence of the established, older critics. All foster the accepted styles; all of the controlling parties have an inherent interest in the status quo.

Because the media are fragmented today, one finds both impressionistic and authoritarian reviews in ample supply. The leading newspapers and magazines tend to offer authoritarian criticism, while television, a more spontaneous and casual medium, appears to generate more impressionistic criticism. In the alternative media, especially urban newspapers catering to the youthful, "hip" counter-culture, columnists and critics such as Harlan Ellison, television reviewer for the Los Angeles *Free Press*, and Jonas Mekas, film writer for the *Village Voice*, offer highly personal and frequently anti-establishment reactions.

THE CASE AGAINST AUTHORITARIANISM

The strongest arguments against the authoritarian position are that it tends to (1) remove the audience from the center and (2) create an atmosphere where the "box score" is the end in itself. The impressionistic review places the audience (represented by the critic) at the center in order to describe and measure its reaction. The authoritarian review, on the other hand, asks the reader to stand by and watch while the critic submits the work to laboratory analysis.

The "box score" mentality comes about because the authoritarian theory generates "hits" and "misses" on a premeasured scale. For example, when a new Edward Albee play opens on Broadway, most of the critics are determined to tell their audience where the career of America's most promising playwright is headed. They compare and contrast his current effort with *Who's Afraid of Virginia Woolf?* Conditioned by stock-market reports, National Football League statistics, Detroit auto sales figures, and television program ratings, the typical American readily accepts the box-score approach. Somewhere along the way, the playwright's theme is lost in the shuffle, even though the issue raised—the meaning of death, perhaps, or changing family relationships—should be of great interest.

THE CASE AGAINST IMPRESSIONISM

The arguments against the impressionistic philosophy are that it (1) promotes cultural anarchy, (2) merely substitutes other criteria in place of historical precedent and (3) opens the way to ego-building on the part of the critic.

Assaying the New Criticism in *Saturday Review*, Granville Hicks warned that in the hands of many teachers it becomes the New Pedantry: "Just as in the old days it was easier to teach biography and history than to teach poetry or fiction, so now it is easier to teach images and symbols. . . . Just as truly as the discussion of historical background, it becomes a way of avoiding the contemplation of literature itself." What Hicks decried is the minute textual analysis that spoils literature in an unceasing search for symbolism and imagery. Such an approach loses sight of the goal of literature, which is to create an experience that might excite, disturb and ultimately satisfy the reader.

Whereas the authoritarian critic draws on the body of knowledge that constitutes his background to make the case for or against a work, the impressionist is, in the words of E. B. White, "watching his reaction to it." That can lead to excesses of ego that are of no benefit to artist or audience. After stepping down as Secretary of State, Dean Rusk defended the stuffy ponderousness of international diplomacy on the grounds that it prevents "accidents of personality." The same might be said in favor of the sometimes remote and scholarly authoritarian approach in contrast to the free-wheeling impressionistic.

COMBINING THE BEST OF BOTH

In practice, most reviewers and critics today tend to fall closer to the middle of the authoritarian-impressionist continuum than to either of the extremes. Most offer brief discussion of precedents, putting the work at hand into some sort of context. Then, reflecting perhaps the general casualness of letters and social behavior today, most feel free to switch into the more comfortable personal essay style, often leading to an "I-like-it-because" conclusion.

FIRST PERSON OR THIRD?

This raises the inevitable question: should a reviewer habitually write in the first or the third person?

Proponents of the authoritarian approach argue that the material should speak for itself, that injecting the personal pronoun "I" somehow compromises the argument by suggesting that the comments are purely personal and negotiable. It is also a long-standing tradition in the world of "objective" journalism to write in the third person, and the tradition has carried over even into signed columns. Many old-school journalists feel uncomfortable writing in the first person.

But there are arguments in favor of taking the wraps off the first person. One, cited earlier in the case of Clive Barnes and his inherited mantle, is precisely in order to strip away some of the awesome power vested in critics on major journals. Another was earlier stated by the venerable George Jean Nathan: "Impersonal criticism is like an impersonal fist fight or an impersonal marriage, and as successful." Many would argue that some of the most enjoyable and instructive reviews to read are those that pit the writer in hand-to-hand combat with the artist, not necessarily in anger, but in such a way as to build strength and create a fuller communion of spirits.

REVIEWING FOR THE MASS MEDIA

Another philosophical issue: should the critic be an "expert" or should he serve as surrogate for the "average man" in the audience? While many reviewers shy away from the "expert" label, most agree that their responsibility is to lead, not merely to participate coequally with the audience. A middle-of-the-road position was outlined by Judith Crist when she wrote: "The critic's job is to put forth an individual viewpoint for his readers to evaluate and react to. That, I think, is his function—to stimulate a response, hopefully favorable or very possibly negative—but a response."

"Every would-be critic must seek his or her role in terms of his or her own personality and outlook," wrote Andrew Sarris in the introduction to his collection of reviews, *Confessions of a Cultist: On the Cinema, 1955–1969*. In addition, it is useful to the critic's audience if he then attempts to summarize the guidelines or standards which frame his attitude.

Miss Crist, for example, explained her approach in an article for *TV Guide*, where her short pieces on films appear regularly. "We each have a standard," she explained. "Mine, for a 'good' movie, requires that the movie fulfill its aspiration and that in the course of that fulfillment it illuminate some facet of experience for me, provide some sort of emotional empathy or tell me something about somebody or something. . . . I think honesty of approach, an assumption that the audience has intelligence, a dash of inspiration and a bit of style are the least I demand of a film."

Admitting that a general theory, the gestalt, had always eluded him, *Esquire* film critic Dwight Macdonald told his readers that early in his career he attempted to draw up a set of guiding principles. But he didn't publish them because they seemed constantly in a state of flux, until eventually they boiled down to such generalities of hindsight that they no longer served to explain his philosophy.

In an installment of *This is Channel 2*, a program designed to give viewers a good look at the inner workings of WCBS-TV in New York City, critic Leonard Harris offered his general formula for judging a play: "What is the play trying to do? Does it succeed, or does it fail? Why?" Those are the questions he tries to answer, and he said he works from the viewpoint of an expert who must first teach, then advise, and finally entertain. "You must turn out an interesting, shall we say, work of art yourself," he concluded.

Whatever his attitude, it is the critic's duty to be accessible, willing to consider his reviews not as a final pronouncement but rather as the opening of dialog between himself and the artists or the audience. He should even be willing to discuss the rationale of the system upon which his judgments are based.

5
The Modus Operandi

Earlier we paid a visit to Culture Gulch in order to examine the role of the reviewer and to assay the arts and entertainment coverage of the typical newspaper. Before discussing the writing of reviews, it is useful to return briefly to Culture Gulch to see how the reviewer deals on a day-to-day basis with the mechanics of his job.

First there is the important matter of obtaining books, theater passes and review tickets in order to have something to review. In the sections which follow, it is assumed that the reviewer is starting from the ground up to establish himself. Ordinarily, of course, he would step into an ongoing operation, but it is helpful to know how the various systems function.

BOOKS

Unlike the other fields covered by the arts and entertainment department of a newspaper, book publishing is not a part of the local scene. There are local sales outlets and regional representatives of the publishers, but decisions regarding review copies are made at headquarter offices in New York, Boston and the few other publishing cities, as well as at the dozens of campuses that have university presses.

To get on the lists for free review copies, start by asking the newspaper's executive editor to list you as the paper's book editor in the next edition of the *Editor & Publisher Yearbook*. That will begin to generate the flow of handouts and books.

Next, obtain a list of U. S. book publishers from the reference librarian and compose a letter of introduction to be sent to all of the major houses and any of the smaller ones whose titles are of interest to your readers. The letter should not introduce you so much as your newspaper (or magazine) and its readership. There are more than 1,700 daily newspapers in the United States; the typical book is sent in advance to perhaps two or three hundred, even fewer for first novels and other titles of limited interest.

The publisher is interested in knowing your paper's circulation, the number of reviews carried regularly, the space and treatment accorded the reviews, and most important of all a general demographic profile of the readers. Needless to say, if your paper is in a college town with two or three good book outlets and has educated, affluent readers, you stand a better chance of getting review copies than does your counterpart in a heavily blue-collar manufacturing city in a region not noted for vigorous book sales.

Many publishers maintain two or three different lists, with the most influential group of papers getting many of the new titles and the lowest rated group receiving only a trickle of reference books, specialty items and potential best sellers. If you have a field of special interest and competence that you hope to dwell upon, or if there are groups of hobbyists in your community which are on the lookout for specialized titles, include the information in your letter to the publishers.

Review copies arrive any time from two to six weeks before publication date. That date is an arbitrary "moment" when the book makes its debut. Frequently the book is placed on sale as soon as copies are received by book stores, so the publication date is mainly for the record. It is nice for reviews to coincide with the publication date, but it is by no means mandatory.

An ersatz "review," mimeographed, double-spaced and prepared in standard newspaper syle, is usually found inside the cover of each review copy. Some editors merely put headlines on the handouts and run them as unsigned reviews—favorable, of course. Others use them for items in book columns, a more honest practice although still a bit too much like puffery. Not all the handouts are blatant attempts to garner free publicity, however. Some contain interesting and pertinent biographical information about the author which can be put to valid use by the reviewer.

Another kind of insert notes the limitations put on the use of the review copy by the publisher. Doubleday's statement is typical: "Special permission is required to quote more than 500 words. No dramatization in lectures, television, or radio is allowed." Few reviews are long enough to warrant inclusion of more than 500 words, and in any case it would probably make for a tiresome review, so the limitation is not a serious one.

It is protocol to send two clippings of your review to the publisher. One is filed for possible publicity use in advertising and jacket blurbs; the other is sent to the author. Needless to say, the wise reviewer sends the clips in regularly to assure a continued flow of books.

The book is retained by the reviewer. As was pointed out earlier, this is often his only "payment" from the book page editor. Although the book may have a value of ten dollars or more, it is given to the newspaper for publicity purposes, not as "payola," and neither party construes such a gift as a compromise of ethics. Recently the Internal Revenue Service attempted to establish that book reviewers must pay taxes on the value of review books, arguing that the material was received in lieu of payment. An outcry from authors, writers, editors and publishers caused the IRS to back down.

One of the concerns of the book page editor, of course, is to obtain illustrative material to enhance his layouts. Some newspapers photograph the dust jackets. Others rely on a staff artist or use appropriate "mood" pictures from a general file. Some of the larger publishers supply photos of authors or copies of illustrations from the books—another point to raise in your letter of introduction if you desire such material.

DRAMA

Since the "national theater" is centered in New York City, a special set of circumstances applies along the Great White Way. Scores of newspaper, broadcast and magazine critics must be accommodated by the major productions, so a recognized system of ranking has been established. Most theaters use the Shubert List (after the prominent family chain of Broadway theaters) of critics—those whose constituency is large enough to rate first-night tickets. The others are relegated to the second night, if there is one.

In cities where only one or two theaters serve road shows and local repertory companies, there are not nearly as many critics and the system is simpler. A press agent or an assistant producer usually contacts the local reviewers a few weeks before opening night. He provides background materials, including publicity stills, and sets up interviews with stars or the director.

In cities large and small, the system for "review comps" is the same when it comes to the actual tickets. It is customary to hold two seats for each reviewer. They are usually on the aisle to facilitate a hasty exit in case the review is written under deadline. Ordinarily it is stipulated that the tickets must be picked up 15 minutes before curtain time; otherwise, they may be sold as "house" seats.

Who occupies the critic's other free seat? Most critics bring their wives. A few prefer to work alone; they turn the second seat back. Occasionally critics take along someone whose reactions they want to see: a child to see the *Nutcracker Suite*, a history buff to help judge the musical *1776*, perhaps a musician to help compensate for the reviewer's deaf ear. One New York critic takes a wide variety of friends to the more than 200 productions he reviews each year, all with the same stipulation: "Don't say a word to me about the show until after I've written my review." Those who violate his stricture are never invited again.

No strings are attached to the complimentary tickets. They are provided as a courtesy, supposedly to ensure that the critic has the hard-to-get opening night tickets and a good view of the stage. Occasionally an editor will question the practice and suggest either that the newspaper pay for the tickets or that the critic dig into his own pocket. But as long as the theater owners and producers understand that good reviews can't be bought, the "comp" system works.

MOVIES

Most movie-house chains and independent owners who show first-run films issue a free pass to each local reviewer. It's valid for one year, and good for any performance except road shows. In most cities, the film critic attends the first regular showing, and his review appears the following day.

In larger cities, previews are frequently arranged. Most of the major distributors have offices in New York and Los Angeles where private screenings are held as much as two months ahead of release in order to facilitate reviews in the national magazines, which have a long lead-time.

Most newspaper critics avoid these screenings, however. Sometimes a film will be altered before final release as a result of preview reaction, and advance reviews may cite elements which no longer exist in the final print. Also, the newspaper critic prefers to see the film with a live audience of typical patrons. Sometimes impressions gained while watching the screen in a tiny, plush screening room along with a handful of pseudosophisticates is nowhere near the same as that experienced in a regular theater.

During the 1960s, the growth of so-called "hard ticket" movies— one showing of a three-hour film each night, at prices double that of an ordinary movie—led naturally to the institution of "review comps" that are passed out on the same system used for theater tickets.

Another practice, fortunately growing rarer all the time, is the theater party preview, where a champagne gala and sometimes even a junket to Hollywood or New York are part of the "opening night" festivities. Most conscientious critics decline to participate, recognizing that the press-agentry could color their impression of the film's true worth.

Television

The television critic usually watches under precisely the same circumstances as the viewing audience: feet up and a bowl of potato chips at his side. But occasionally the networks, especially the Public Broadcasting Service, schedule previews in their studios, enabling the critics to alert the audience ahead of time.

The television networks are among the most vigorous promoters of their wares. The entertainment editor is usually inundated with features and publicity stills, especially in the fall, when new shows open, and prior to the holidays, when there are dozens of entertainment specials.

Most other forms of art and entertainment follow one or a combination of the systems outlined above for helping the critic to do his job. Even the Ringling Brothers-Barnum and Bailey Circus bids the ladies and gentlemen of the press to dress up in black tie and enjoy box seats, followed by drinks and a buffet supper attended by the top stars of the spectacle.

In his dealings with others, the critic must have a well-formulated notion of the ethics of his job. Several areas should be cited.

RELATIONSHIPS WITH ARTISTS AND PERFORMERS

Some reviewers are awestruck in the presence of stars, or become self-important because of their familiarity with entertainers. It shows in their reviews. They become unconscious flacks for every performer they meet. Or, worse, they take a superior and condescending attitude toward the lowly reader who is not so fortunate as to mix with the stars.

Occasionally a reviewer with performing in his background is biased toward or against those who practice the same art. He may favor all tenors because he was a tenor once, or conversely he may come down unnecessarily hard on all set designers because he was the world's most promising set designer back in his college days.

In dealing with those he judges—and most critics meet and know those who are the objects of their scrutiny—the critic must understand the dynamics of his own personality so that he can counterbalance tendencies to become either a fan or a persecutor.

In the night club world of intimate, live performances, for example, the singer or musician frequently joins the gentlemen of the press at ringside between shows. The exchange can give the reviewer insight regarding the performer's personality and objective. It can also lead to fistfights. Or free drinks and an undeserved rave review.

RELATIONSHIP WITH THE MOVERS AND SHAKERS

Equally brimming with promise and fraught with peril are the contacts that develop with leaders of the cultural community, the business community and sometimes even politicians. When the critic attempts to perform his role as promoter of culture, he becomes involved—whether he likes it or not—with high-pressure types who are accustomed to getting what they want, and paying for it, or bringing their considerable powers to bear if necessary. Many of them haven't heard about the Canons of Journalism.

Suffice it to say that the writer who becomes the tool of Mrs. Big and her society cronies has diminished his usefulness as a judge of what is truly good. Long before the critic feels pressure building, he has the responsibility of tactfully educating the movers and shakers of the community regarding his role and that of his newspaper. In the long run, the community's cultural needs will be better served.

RELATIONSHIP WITH ADVERTISERS

There have been numerous occasions on which producers—or at least people working for producers—have pulled advertising following an unfavorable review. Judith Crist's stinging criticism reportedly cost the *New York Herald Tribune* $250,000 in revenue during its final months. Sometimes the act is accompanied by a threat that "We'll never advertise in this paper again, or at least not as long as so-and-so is the critic."

No newspaper needs a four-by-four inch advertisement one tenth as much as the producer needs the exposure in the community's leading medium of communication. Typically, the enraged advertiser stays away no longer than a few weeks, or until he has a new production that needs promotion. The advertising manager, reluctant to lose any account, may feel strongly enough to confront the executive editor with the heated letter of complaint. On a good newspaper, the critic may not even get involved in the brouhaha, unless a copy of the letter of complaint is addressed to him. If he is contacted, he should merely explain his function in brief, and then refer the matter to the top editor. The editors, in turn, should send the complainant to the advertising department, where the matter belongs. If, on a lesser journal, the critic feels any pressure at all, he would be well advised to seek employment elsewhere. To permit advertisers to dictate content is to compromise the entire concept of the critical review.

It should be pointed out that most newspapers are established as profit-making enterprises deriving the bulk of their income from the selling of advertising space. The critic who wages a concerted campaign against commercial interests or appears to go out of his way to ascribe fault to everything the local promoters do may find himself out of step with the publisher's aims. It has happened more than once, and it usually results in a job opening.

Relationship with one's own newspaper

Critics are not like other newspapermen. They wear pressed suits and shined shoes. They make their own hours, built around the theater schedules. They don't write their copy in inverted pyramids, but rather in essay form. And they scream bloody murder if one little paragraph is cut from the end of their piece. Thus there is a strong tendency for critics to become outcasts.

Here are a few commandments to the reviewer who finds himself walking through the newsroom in a state of complete invisibility: Thou shalt not take a back seat to other departments, but neither shalt thou get preferential treatment. Thou shalt make an attempt to understand the problems of, and communicate with, the harried editors around the copy desk. Thou shalt not be disloyal to thine own newspaper in public, thus poisoning thine own mind, as well as thine own reputation, in the process.

Unfortunately many of the inhabitants of Culture Gulch who are otherwise superior persons can't bring themselves to keep these three simple commandments.

Relationship with public relations men

Public relations is an accepted, and pervasive, part of life in America. It is impossible for a reviewer to state unconditionally that he will never allow himself to be approached by a PR man. If a theater owner puts out a tray of canapés during the intermission, it's absurd to assume that a smidgeon of liver pâté or a cold shrimp will transform a pan into a rave. In a country where expense account lunches are a way of life, letting a producer pick up the tab shouldn't taint the writer's reputation.

Most newspapers prohibit gifts of any kind for their newsroom employees, except for such innocent items as imprinted ballpoint pens and desk calendars. But press agents are constantly finding ways to get around the rule. A few years ago one of the television networks put out a voluminous packet of promotional material on its fall programs. It was delivered personally to the television editors of hundreds of newspapers in a standard attaché case with colorful stick-on labels proclaiming the network's slogan for the new season. It didn't take much wisdom to see that, once the handouts were removed and the stickers peeled off the outside, the editor had himself a very nice $35 personal item. Many kept them; some merely left them on top of their file cabinets for months to follow. Very few complained.

The most blatant form of seduction is the junket. When 20th Century-Fox previewed *The Flim-Flam Man*, the studio invited several dozen entertainment editors to Louisville, Kentucky, over Derby Day weekend. The articles, features and interviews that followed—and not a few of the reviews, as well—were positively rapturous. That's some flim-flam. Metro-Goldwyn-Mayer flew 200 newsmen into New York for a party at the Rainbow Room, guest tickets to all the hit shows, a free boat ride and, incidentally, a preview of *The Dirty Dozen*. Earl Wilson headlined his subsequent column: "MGM Is 'Santa' to 200 Newsmen." That may or may not have had some bearing on the fact that the movie was a big hit at the box office. But, doubtless, it raised the question in the minds of many readers of whether reviews and stories in the news media are any different from paid advertisements.

Anyone involved in reviewing and criticism or coverage of the arts and entertainment has to be rather like a saint: willing to absorb the multitudinous minor assaults on his vulnerability while holding steadfastly to the principle of refusing to sell his judgment at any price.

6
Put It
in Writing:
The Vital Lead

In a typical scholarly journal, where the contributors are mostly Ph.D.s, every other book review begins "This book . . ." and ends ". . . worthy addition to any bookshelf." Not much has changed since the third grade, when each oral book report began, "I like this book because . . ."

The world of culture is heavily populated with authorities and experts, but few effective critics. The main reason is that evaluations, however thoughtful and valid, must be translated from mind to paper. The process is difficult. Much is lost in the act of communication if the writer does not have a knack for presentation.

Instead of calling the material in this chapter a guide to *writing* reviews, let's consider it a discussion of how to *present* information and ideas effectively. Writing ability derives from a combination of factors, including talent, style and personal orientation—items no book can readily alter for the reader. But techniques and examples can be examined profitably, with an eye toward finding modes which serve the beginner and help him to develop as a critical writer.

There is no set way to write a critical notice, but you might not know that if you followed the work of certain reviewers. A great number of persons assume, perhaps because of the rules set down by generations of high school English teachers, that one offers a full plot summary followed by a sentence assigning the appropriate adjective to each of the aspects of the work at hand.

Sometimes even the best writers are forced, because of space limitations, to merely tick off the winners and sinners—the good points and the bad. But when it becomes a consistent device the resulting reviews are reduced to the level of statistical tables. They might as well be set up like racing results or college basketball standings. Here, for example, is how a television reviewer attempted to summarize a Diana Ross special:

> The singing by Miss Ross and the Jackson Five was great; the sets were handsome; Miss Ross's clothes were stunning. The comedy was terrible, even with the help of Bill Cosby and Danny Thomas.

"Great, handsome, stunning and terrible" just don't say much. On the other hand, the straight list can occasionally be used effectively to indicate an overwhelming quality about a work. Here is how the same television reviewer attempted to show the scope of a John Wayne special:

> Johnny Cash, Leslie Uggams and Roy Clark sang. Ann-Margret danced. Dennis Weaver played Abe Lincoln's father. Bing Crosby was made up to look like Mark Twain and talked about the brotherhood of man. Wayne got into the saddle once and then roamed around a ghost town talking about the good old days. The Boston Tea Party was staged; a huge set showing the United States split in half to show the Civil War. It was all on a very large scale.

The super-paragraph did convey the feeling of plenty going on, and it doubtless would have been impossible in the space allotted to discuss the various segments in any depth. Note, however, that the format appears to spawn dull writing: "The Boston Tea Party *was staged*" (passive voice); "a huge set *showing* . . . split in half to *show* . . ." (word repetition).

The plot summary is sometimes justified. Situations which call for full expositions of the story line include those in which:

(1) The story is not nearly as important as another facet of the work, so to reveal it in its entirety in no way reduces the audience's enjoyment of the work. Most opera and ballet plots, for example,

can be told without "ruining the ending" for anyone. In fact, a large segment of the mass audience, unfamiliar with all but the most popular and well-known operas and ballets, would probably be enlightened and assisted by an explanation.

(2) The genesis of a book lies in a true incident unfamiliar to most readers. In order to establish the magnitude of the event, the reviewer condenses the story and includes enough documentation to convince the reader of its authenticity. If the story is intriguing or important enough, the reader's appetite is whetted, and he seeks out the book in order to receive fuller details and documentation. Authors happily employ this technique in their appearances on the late-night television talk shows, with no loss of sales.

(3) The reviewer cannot make criticisms of substance unless the reader is acquainted with the thrust of the story. This reasoning leads critics to summarize the plots of films and plays, despite the fact that it may lessen the desire of potential audience members, who then know "how it turns out." When the critic does tell all, it is often because the resolution of the plot is unreasonable, or because the reason for creating the work is, after all, invalid.

(4) The work depicts the life of a famous person whose story is familiar to everyone. The reviewer recounts it as a reminder and as a way of injecting tangential information.

When mystery or suspense is the key element, revealing the ending is bad form. Although it is difficult to resist repeating the best lines from a Neil Simon comedy or the funniest incidents in a Woody Allen movie, doing so often detracts from the audience's enjoyment. Better to select adjectives which *categorize* mystery or humor than to attempt to recapture the best moments of a work.

A final argument against plot summaries is that they can easily become boring. Often much of a work's texture is lost in condensation, and all that is left is meaningless bare-bones structure. The tendency is to glue it together with repetitions of "then . . . and then . . . and then. . . ." The critical review is essentially an essay, and its form does not lend itself to the capsulizing of long works.

An obvious exception is the review that parodies a work, offering nothing but the plot retold in a mocking or disapproving way. *Time* magazine, with its penchant for cynicism and wordplays, occasionally pulls off a parody review with great success.

If plot summaries and box scores are not always the best way to organize a review, what is the most acceptable alternative? The answer is found in the word "essay," which *A Dictionary of Literary Terms* defines as "a composition having no pretensions to completeness or thoroughness of treatment." It comes from the French word *essai*, or attempt. In other words, a review is a short attempt to assess a work in a way that is interesting, though not encyclopedic. The writer must calculate an approach which he feels will get him easily into the topic, allow him to advance some ideas and record some observations while exploring it, and then permit him to exit gracefully, leaving fuller exposition until another time and perhaps in another medium.

The opening sentences or paragraph of any journalistic piece is called the "lead." In a review, which is not bound completely to journalistic style, the concept of the attention-grabbing, topic-setting lead is relaxed considerably. We may consider the first few paragraphs to be the lead or introductory segment.

In the pages that follow, we shall examine a number of these segments to understand the ways in which a review might be conceived and presented.

Alerting the fans

For the fans who enjoy high pressure suspense-adventure stories, here is the latest offering from MacLean, a very successful practitioner of the art—as evidenced by such previous works as the *Navarone* novels and the more recent *Puppet on a Chain*. (Miles A. Smith, A. P. critic, reviewing *Caravan to Vaccares* by Alistair MacLean in *The Home News*, New Brunswick, New Jersey.)

At first glance, this might appear to be a cliché lead. Fill in the blanks: "For fans who enjoy such-and-such, here is such-and-such." Indeed, it is closely related to the hackneyed "recipe" lead: "Take a little such-and-such, add a dash of such-and-such, plus a pinch of such-and-such, and you have such-and-such."

But the reviewer has provided a useful service. He has alerted us to the fact that this book is aimed at the faithful audience of a particular genre, in this case suspense-adventure. The opening words—"For the fans who"—are the tipoff, and the categorization follows immediately. Perhaps three fourths of the newspaper's readers will spin out before the end of the lead, and contrary to the usual journalistic standards it's just as well. Westerns, mysteries, gothic romances and hobby books have their devotees. Others are not likely to be interested in even a brief review.

In the three paragraphs following the lead, the reviewer discusses the plot and the protagonist. His fifth and final stanza summarizes: "Perhaps MacLean has laid it on a bit thick this time, but that's the way a real adventure fan expects it to be." Thus the premise of the lead is further amplified.

Promoting the author

Marge Piercy looks young and round and pretty and has a head full of flying bricks, and anyone who wants to learn what the revolution against the fat society is all about should read her novels. Those not beguiled by the revolution should read her novels anyway. (John Skow reviewing *Dance the Eagle to Sleep* by Marge Piercy in *Time*.)

This ebullient approach attempts to overwhelm the reader with the reviewer's enthusiasm for the author following his reading of her latest book. It might result in a rush to the bookstores, but it could just as easily backfire. The unrestrained rave denies the reader the pleasure of absorbing the review, weighing the evidence, and making his own choice.

Even the author might be embarrassed by the gushy lead above; she'd probably be just as happy to see the same sentiment expressed toward the end of the essay, after the reader had had a chance to warm to the book. The argument in favor of such an enthusiastic beginning is that critics too often dissect a work in cold, clinical terms. Occasionally it's healthy and reassuring to see a critic give rein to his emotions and endorse an artist unreservedly.

Confessing a bias

Here on home grounds I had better begin my review of Andrew Sarris's collected film criticism by making my own confession that I have never been a devotee of his or even a regular reader. (Richard Gilman reviewing *Confessions of a Cultist: On the Cinema, 1955–1969* by Andrew Sarris in *The Village Voice*.)

The very least one can say for this beginning is that it is honest and forthright. It is also intensely personal, a hallmark of *The Village Voice* and other alternative media. Not all book reviewers are able to be as honest: the prolific writer Herbert Gold, in an *Atlantic* article, recalled the time a book editor would not permit him to say that he was a personal friend of the author whose work he was reviewing. "We don't admit friendship plays any part in reviewing," Gold quotes the editor. "If it does, we don't admit it."

Reviews by acquaintances (or, conversely, by rivals) of an author are not uncommon. In specialized professional fields, frequently only a few colleagues are capable of reviewing a technical book. In smaller cities and towns, the reviewer is bound to know the local authors about whom he must write. And in the leading book review supplements the practice of playing off friends, rivals and competitors is assumed to generate lively, provocative reviews that may signal the beginning of an interesting debate. The editor who condones the cover-up is narrow minded and unimaginative as well as dishonest.

A group of college students to whom the above lead was read was almost unanimously intrigued by it. "There's a promise of interesting conflict," said one. "I detect a very complimentary review in the offing, despite the disclaimer," observed another. Indeed, the long review (3,300 words—another *Village Voice* trait is a reluctance to bridle its writers) came quickly to the conclusion that Sarris and his theories were worthy of "solid respect," if not enthusiasm. And the essay, true to the promise of the lead, gave adequate background material to demonstrate why Sarris has his devotees and his detractors.

Personalizing an anecdote

Do you know why the page you're reading now is the size it is? Answer: It's a tax dodge. When British newspapers were taxed by the page in 1712, printers were quick to figure out they could pay less tax and publish more news by using huge pages. Those taxes disappeared more than a century ago, but readers—and machines—were accustomed to handling big pages, and they stayed. Next question: Will you be folding and unfolding pages like this 20 years from this morning—or will computerized news be transmitted by coaxial cable to your home, where you'll make copies of the items you want to examine, then press a button for further information? (Walter Clemons reviewing *The Information Machines* by Ben H. Bagdikian in *The New York Times*.)

Put It in Writing: The Vital Lead

The Bagdikian book combines journalism history, incisive criticism of a field steeped in tradition (much of it smug) and a look into the future of mass communications. The reviewer neatly ties all these aspects together with his opening gambit.

What is more important, he focuses the initial segment on the reader and his concerns. The topic might easily have led to a dry or lofty examination of some aspect of the institution rather than to the impact of the institution on the individual. Media critic Bagdikian should be pleased to see the reviewer "localizing" the material, fitting it to his reader's concerns and interests.

EVALUATING IN RETROSPECT

Ronald Reagan described San Francisco State College as a 'domestic Vietnam' during the 5-month strike that transformed the campus into a battleground during late 1968 and early 1969. The California governor might have been guilty of a rare understatement. For the forces unleashed at San Francisco State in the '60s may well be with us long after the wars on the Indo-Chinese peninsula are a faded nightmare. (James Brann reviewing *An End to Silence: The San Francisco State Student Movement in the '60s* by Barlow and Shapiro in the *Washington Post.*)

Another tenet of effective mass communication is that a punchy, active, interesting word or phrase should begin the lead sentence, rather than a dull opening such as "There is . . ." or "Back in 1968, when . . ." Considering that the very name of California's tough-minded governor is bound to strike a vein of intense feeling one way or the other, this beginning is an attention getter.

Further, it provides the reader with enough brief clues or reminders for him to recall the campus tribulations of a few years before. This was the issue, the reviewer points out later, that made S. I. Hayakawa a household word.

The effect of the third sentence is twofold. On one hand, it pointedly summarizes the importance of the book's topic, at least in the estimate of the reviewer. But an appreciable number of college writing students who were asked to comment on the lead segment said that phrases such as "forces unleashed" and "faded nightmare" ring of jingoism, thus possibly diminishing the interest of potential readers who feel they have been told much too often about crises in politics, education, world affairs and social welfare.

ATTACKING A CONVENTION

Contrary to popular opinion, a literary reputation is one of the hardest things in the world to lose. Once among the elect, a novelist is as difficult to impeach as a president. (Anatole Broyard reviewing *The Onion Eaters* by J. P. Donleavy in *The New York Times*.)

Reviewer Broyard, one of the most incisive writers to grace the pages of the *Times* or any other paper in any capacity, found Donleavy's fifth novel abominable: "In 306 pages of straining for effect, there has not been a believable character, a meaningful incident, a good laugh, an interesting observation or an admirable sentence." The reviewer's three-paragraph condensation of the strained, often ludicrous incidents that comprise the story tends to confirm the judgment for the reader.

But before getting around to those observations Broyard addresses himself to the phenomenon of the "irrevocable reputation" enjoyed by authors whose good fortune it was to have a successful first novel. This is a legitimate topic, for even readers who will never read a word of Donleavy have at times wondered aloud: "How does a book like this get published?" The answer, according to the reviewer, lies in the vagaries of book publishing; uncertain editors are willing to ride with a former winner, although the manuscript in hand is unfathomable.

When a book makes no sense at all, Broyard concludes, confused reviewers describe it as "bursting the confines of the conventional novel." In this piece, however, the reviewer is the fellow who dares say the emperor is as naked as the day he was born.

APPLAUDING THE TECHNIQUE

I was trying to plow right through 'Home Life' in order to get my review in on time, but it was impossible. Every few pages, I had to stop and admire the book—or simply sit back and feel it. My God, but my fellow creatures are fascinating! I found myself thinking. How touching, how absurd, how real they are! All at once I was delighted to be sharing their destiny. (Anatole Broyard reviewing *Home Life, A Story of Old Age* by Rabinowitz and Neilson in *The New York Times*.)

Conversely—and happily—the same reviewer is capable of experiencing exactly the opposite reaction. His admiration is expressed here in a way that is not corny or embarrassing but genuinely appreciative of the rare authors who can move their readers to touch and feel and know the characters they have created.

Often when a reviewer injects himself and his work into his reviews, the result is egocentric shoptalk. Here the sheer sincerity of the writer prevents any such interpretation, and the device is not offensive.

CHALLENGING THE PREMISE

No fuss. No bother. Eliminate dirty smudges on the fingertips, broken nails, and messy erasure marks. You don't need to revise, rethink, or rewrite. You don't even need to write. Just think of it, folks: No more bloodshot eyes, or coffee bowels, or angry friends you've stood up to work just a little longer, harder, more. Sealed inside your own angry mortal human vacuum, to be just as fatuous as Margaret Mead and James Baldwin about the crisis of our time—particularly race—all you have to do is talk and not listen, always avoid expressing your feelings openly, refer constantly to other times and other cultures with historical and/or pseudohistorical truths, interrupt whenever possible, call yourself a prophet or a poet, insist that you are being emotionally sincere and/or objectively rational, and record it all on tape, to be transcribed later as a book. (Richard Elman reviewing *A Rap on Race* by Mead and Baldwin in the Sunday *New York Times*.)

Whereas the review of *The Onion Eaters* focuses on a fiction book-trade phenomenon, this essay in the Sunday book section attacked the method of "assembling" a nonfiction book marketed at $6.95. The reviewer's concern is legitimate. Anthropologist Mead's previous book, priced at $5.00, was but a reprint of a lecture series. The manuscript, augmented with various appendixes, barely exceeded 100 pages when set in extremely large type on small pages with generous margins. The reader received no more of the author's time, energy and ideas than would the reader of one of her articles in a 50¢ magazine.

Bookmaking schemes' aside, the ideas generated by the conversations between the authors also failed to impress the reviewer; he attacked them throughout his essay. It is interesting to note that reviewers who found the ideas useful did not attack the concept or the format of the book. The reviewer for the daily *Times* had no quibble with the method; he merely mentioned the technique in one short, noncommittal sentence.

SATIRIZING THE STYLE

NORA: One morning The Times Book Review called and asked us if we'd review *The Couple*, the story of a married couple who went to the Masters and Johnson Clinic in St. Louis to solve their sex problems. The book already had 60,000 copies in print before publication and was scheduled for major promotion and advertising. I told them to send it over.

DAN: The book arrived, and . . .

(Nora Ephron and Dan Greenburg reviewing *The Couple* in *The New York Times*.)

Riding the lucrative tide of nonfiction sex primers by authors with only initials for names, *The Couple* was bound to be panned in many quarters. Humorist Greenberg and his wife did it by satirizing perfectly the husband-wife, back-and-forth format of the book. All necessary information is incorporated in their deadpan dialog. The result is devastatingly effective—and a welcome change in the too often superserious book review pages.

LEADING WITH A SUMMARY

Without any ands, ifs or buts, let it be said that Pierre Salinger has written a superior suspense novel that is thoroughly absorbing, splendidly plotted and scrupulously written. And he has done it by making the suspense derive not from gore, mayhem and derring-do, although the book has its share of these, but from the hazards of political maneuvering, the clash of ideologies and from the natural complexity that is inherent in all human situations. (Thomas Lask reviewing *On Instructions of My Government* by Pierre Salinger in *The New York Times*.)

Although the two sentences launch a 750-word review, they could easily stand alone; certainly they serve the hasty reader who has time only to skim, for here is a complete summary that lists all of the book's strong points. Of course such an approach is easiest in the case of an unqualified rave or an unmitigated pan.

Some papers request that reviewers hand in two versions of each book review, one of standard length and the other in capsule form—as short as 50 words. The editor then can make effective use of the materials available to him by using miniversions as fillers around the reviews he feels are worth full treatment. This lead, like that of a good news story, could serve either purpose.

ANALYZING THE GENRE

The promise of *cinéma vérité* is that it holds the mirror up to nature without any refraction imposed by the script or interpreters. Its problem is that the very presence of a camera and, later, the act of editing what the camera has observed inevitably lead to some degree of distortion. Both the promise and the problem are fascinatingly apparent in Allan King's new film, *A Married Couple.* (Roland Gelatt reviewing *A Married Couple* in *Saturday Review.*)

Frequently the comments and criticisms that a reviewer wishes to make are esoteric unless the hallmarks of the special genre are familiar to the readers. Hence the opening segment of this essay constitutes a miniature lesson wherein the writer imparts the necessary comprehension. In the past decade, only one or two films shown each year (and then usually only in the large cities) used the techniques of *cinéma vérité*, so Gelatt and many other reviewers of *A Married Couple* focused on this aspect.

On the stage, melodrama and the musical comedy are as American as apple pie, but other forms are less familiar to the average audience. So when *What the Butler Saw* played Washington, D. C., Richard Lebherz, reviewer for the Frederick, Md., *Post*, devoted a large part of his review to enumerating the ingredients of farce. Asserting that American audiences have trouble dealing with farce, he explained that audiences in countries that have long histories—and the resulting detachment and assuredness—appreciate farce better than citizens of younger nations. His ideas may have frightened some of the audience away, but those who did see the play probably understood it better and appreciated it more than if they had gone in cold.

NOTING THE TREND

As young people become more restive and their politics more violent, movies about them become more offensive, condescending and dishonest. Some invidious ratio is at work here, witness the latest entry in the let's-make-money-off-the-kids sweepstakes, Stanley Kramer's *R.P.M.* (Jay Cocks reviewing *R.P.M.* in *Time.*)

Had it been the first of the "campus unrest" movies, Kramer's film probably would still have rated Judith Crist's favorite adjective: banal. Coming as it did in the wake of *The Revolutionary, The Strawberry Statement, Wild in the Streets* and several lesser films, its mediocrity made it quite redundant.

What's more, *Time*'s reviewer sees a trend, and he feels that it is important to blow the whistle on that Frankenstein creation before dealing with the work at hand. Warning the townspeople is the first step when any monster is loose. His work is bound to be unending, of course, for Hollywood insists on replicating last year's box office success *ad infinitum*.

ACKNOWLEDGING THE REPUTATION

Once in a while a movie arrives amidst such vile notoriety and rumblings of fiasco that it is almost impossible to show up at the screening without a dark sense of foreboding or long thoughts about putting in for a transfer to sports. (Charles Champlin reviewing *Rabbit, Run* in the *Los Angeles Times*.)

Reviewer Champlin is discussing the film made from the best-selling John Updike book of the same name. It was one of those movies that drew jeers at its preview, so the distributor dumped dozens of prints on secondary markets and hoped to recoup part of his costs before any of the big-time media grew wise. (It was not reviewed in New York or in the national magazines.) *Casino Royale*, with its midstream director changes, and *Myra Breckenridge*, with its lurid rumors from the casting couch and the set, had wretched reputations far in advance of the first screening. Only *Casino Royale*, with too many presold ingredients to flop completely, managed to get a decent run at theaters around the country.

Is the reviewer lowering himself to the level of a gossip columnist when he acknowledges the rumors and the trade talk about a work? Should he ignore such information and judge the piece strictly on its merits? It would be gratifying to be able to give an unreserved "yes" to these double-edged questions. And, indeed, some of the most respected reviewers—Kael of *The New Yorker*, Kauffman of *The New Republic*—often manage to pitch their commentary at a level that ignores the skirmishes below.

But the ordinary reviewer finds it hard to do. After all, his readers are aware of the advance billing; they listen to Rona Barrett on Metromedia; they subscribe to *Life,* and *Pageant,* and *Silver Screen;* their local newspaper carries all the NEA and WNS goodies with Hollywood datelines. To write for this audience in apparent ignorance of "what they're all saying about Liz and Dick" may undercut the writer's reputation as an authority on the movies.

On a more serious level, suppose the damaging advance publicity has appeared only in the trade papers and among the cognoscenti? In such instances, it's more a matter of judgment on the reviewer's part. If the advance reputation appears to have been justified, and if the reasons explain the current condition of the film, using the information is quite justified. Once in a while the rumors are wrong. Sometimes they are even *favorable* rumors. But longtime critics will confirm that more often than not the mackerel that smells bad when it comes into the house is going to taste bad when it's served.

Appraising the transition

The movie industry's addi..ion to picaresque fictions seems as much a bid for temporary survival as it does an appreciation of a culturally current form. To a large degree a reflection of the kinds of novels that have been published in the last few years, the picaresque movie usually finds itself trying to answer the question: 'What do we do when we haven't got a story?' What we do, of course, is pretend we didn't want a story—and then fill up the empty places with charm. (Roger Greenspun reviewing *Pigeons* in *The New York Times.*)

The vast majority of American films are based on stories told first in other media, mainly novels and stage plays. Similarly, most Broadway entries in recent years have been adaptations, revivals and imports. The film and drama reviewers, therefore, must be familiar with the original story sources, and their reviewing task is often one of detailing the reason for a successful or unsuccessful voyage across the treacherous waters from one specialized medium to another equally specialized medium.

Pigeons was based on the David Boyer novel *The Sidelong Glances of a Pigeon Kicker,* which is a fair title for a work of fiction but far too obscure to go up in lights on a marquee in Keokuk, Iowa. Only the film with its streamlined title probably won't even play Keokuk, since the reviewer makes it clear that the transition from printed page to silver screen didn't work.

What makes a good critic is not just depth, then, but breadth as well. In one season a film reviewer is going to see movies based on best-selling novels of adventure and intrigue, obscure novels of self-examination, blockbuster musicals, a Pinter play, perhaps even a headache commercial or a collection of graffiti. It stands to reason that his interests have to be eclectic, and it will help if he has some familiarity across the board. That familiarity should include the basic techniques of each medium. He understands and appreciates, for example, how a novelist uses dialog to create a certain kind of tension between characters, while the filmmaker creates an analogous sort of tension by using camera angles, selective focus and the accentuation of visual mannerisms. The astute reviewer speaks half a dozen languages and is able to translate as readily as a UN guide. It's another manifestation of his role as instructor.

Isolating a symptom

The single gesture that amused me most during Peter Brook's new staging of *A Midsummer Night's Dream* may have been inadvertent, though I don't think it was. It came when Bottom, devoutly rehearsing his play and finding himself under prim instruction from Quince to play a scene a certain way, went ahead and did it Quince's way but kept shaking his head all the while. Actors *will* do that—follow directions dutifully while making it perfectly clear that they are in no way responsible for the crime—and I laughed aloud at the sight of it. I may also have been taken with the moment because it reflected, in miniature, my own feelings about Mr. Brook's trapeze-haunted production of Shakespeare's idyll: I accepted what was being given me without ever quite seeing the sense of it. (Walter Kerr reviewing *A Midsummer Night's Dream* in *The New York Times*.)

The above opening segment is quintessential Kerr, at least as he approaches things in his current incarnation as a Sunday essayist. Kerr never seems to focus on scripts or sets or actors' whole bodies anymore. He seizes upon an entrance, a raised finger, a facial expression and, like a scientist who has discovered a tiny telltale growth in his agar, he rushes to the microscope and the dissecting table.

A penchant for minutiae can be irritating in a second-rate critic. An entire play isn't built around a lisp, a wink or a twitch, so why reverse the process, boiling the whole kettle's worth of drama away until only the wink or the twitch is left? A reviewer occasionally tries the "minute detail" approach because he is unable to sum up the whole in any other terms. Perhaps the meaning or the worth of the play escaped him entirely, so he covers up his ignorance (or, charitably, his lapse) with an essay on acting nuances or, in films, editing techniques.

Kerr isn't usually guilty of that. A teachery critic whose books (*How Not to Write a Play* is one) are studied by would-be play-wrights, he can deliver a useful and valid lecture on any of the parts that make up the whole play. While any writer is capable of writing a piece about new faces in the theater, Kerr's essay will be called "The Stage Face," and it will go beyond the superficial to discuss the special qualities that lift one aspiring actor above the crowd of a thousand, making him a stage presence and ultimately a star.

Vincent Canby, Kerr's film counterpart, strives to do the same for his medium. A woman sitting near him in the theater whispers to no one in particular that Warren Beatty "looks just like Jesus!" during a moment of *McCabe and Mrs. Miller.* Canby seizes upon it as a telling observation: "Shots that make the characters look just like Jesus don't happen by accident," he assures his readers. And that anecdote is sufficient to hang a review on, for the main problem Canby finds with Robert Altman's film is that it is too often heavy handed with symbolism. The film is so busy making historical and contemporary allusions that the narrative drive is undercut, Canby feels.

In the hands of a fine critic, and if used sparingly, the approach is one that an intelligent reader can appreciate.

SETTING THE MOOD

The Ronald Millar stage version of the medieval love story *Abelard and Heloise* begins and ends in a monastery. Although their story is told as a flashback in the middle portion of the play, spiritually the production never leaves the austere, restrained place of retreat. It seems an unlikely setting for one of the world's great love stories. (Ernest Albrecht reviewing *Abelard and Heloise* in *The Home News,* New Brunswick, New Jersey.)

Many of the *Abelard and Heloise* reviews began with a brief re-telling of the classic love story. Albrecht, a thoughtful and intelligent reviewer for a small daily, might well have taken the standard route. But he felt it was important to focus on the way of telling the story rather than the story itself.

Everything in the writing of the first paragraph serves that end. The sentences, like the subject they describe, are austere and restrained. The style is downbeat: only the word "flashback" is sharp edged. The writer wasn't straining for the effect; it reflects his own mood at the time he left the theater . . . the opposite side of the coin from the ebullient, zestful words that spring from the typewriter when the critic has just been ignited by a barnburner of a musical.

The final phrase of the full review tells us that the play was "less moving than it might be, and inconsistently engaging." Unlike some reviews that appear to end up talking about quite another production than the one referred to at the beginning, Albrecht's piece is consistent throughout.

CAPTURING THE GLITTER

PALM BEACH—Alan Ayckbourn's London hit, *How the Other Half Loves*, at the Royal Poinciana Playhouse in its American premiere Monday captivated its opening night crowd, many of them socialites, and proved a brilliant boulevard comedy. (Review of *How the Other Half Loves* in the *Miami Herald*.)

There's a fatal tipoff in the lead written by this "correspondent" (as opposed to reviewer) for the Miami paper. We are told, with obvious relish and infatuation, that the audience was heavily laden with socialites.

The remainder of the review was an embarrassing rave. Embarrassing because words like "great" and "completely absorbing theater" and "merry mixup" and "terrific" are squandered the way a Palm Beach socialite tosses around her husband's money on a boulevard shopping spree. This lead signals that a society page item has gone visiting in the entertainment pages.

FOCUSING ON THE INSTITUTION

Although its charter is primarily to educate the young, The Juilliard School now and then extends its franchise to graduates, post-graduates, and even non-graduates in need of the kind of illumination it dispenses. The latest in a long sequence of such services was a production of Mozart's all but legendary *La Clemenza di Tito* in the attractive Juilliard

Theater, with Bruno Maderna conducting a production designed by John Scheffler and directed by Osvaldo Riofrancos for the American Opera Center (a Juilliard subsidiary). (Irving Kolodin in *Saturday Review*.)

Occasionally it is not so important to analyze a work as it is to comment upon its reason for being, or sometimes even the *raison d'être* behind the institution which presents it to the public. Here the magazine reviewer prefaces his discussion of the work with what he feels is necessary background on the Juilliard facilities.

Similarly, New York papers ran leads like this one for a production of *Timon of Athens:* "Free Shakespeare is back in Central Park, so summer must have started." The focus was on Joseph Papp's frequently beleaguered Shakespeare Festival Public Theater. Its funding, its choice of plays and its tenuous existence had to be treated before judging the play at hand. In this case, the critics were not pleased with the play ("When a play by Shakespeare is lesser there is usually a very good reason for it") but they defended Papp's decision to perform it because of the special responsibility of a grant-supported institution to include both obscure works and old favorites in its repertoire.

Perhaps one reason so many of the leading mass media reviewers have backgrounds in journalism as well as in the art fields they write about is that editors want people who can estimate the news value of a cultural event and present "coverage" along with comment.

7
Avoiding
the Cliché

Never wish an actor good luck on opening night: theater legend holds that it's a curse, sure to bring disaster. Instead, "Break a leg" is the customary admonition.

By the same token, talking about "style"—while it would seem central to any discussion of writing skills—is usually counterproductive. What, after all, is a writing style? Is there really any way it can be systematically measured, categorized, evaluated or rated? Injecting a question about "style" into a writers' conference is more mischievous than turning a mouse loose at a D.A.R. meeting: the ladies only scream and scatter; the writers argue pointlessly for hours about adjectives, imagery and ideal sentence length.

Beginning reviewers would be better off avoiding grand discussions of "style," directing their attention instead toward two facets of writing which are crucial to effective criticism: avoiding the cliché, and condensing description.

Avoiding the cliché is a simple matter—or so it would seem to the earnest beginner. But the cliché is an insidious beast, lurking in the shadows, waiting to take advantage of any sign of fatigue or laziness on the writer's part. There is even a school of thought which holds that the people who build typewriters actually program clichés, bromides and worn-out phrases into their machines, especially the electric models. The unsuspecting writer who leans on the space bar while searching for an adjective may unwittingly trip the lock, permitting an entire pack of offenders to escape and arrange themselves across the empty expanses of copy paper. Eternal vigilance is the price of excellent writing.

The following movie review is reprinted exactly as it appeared in a newspaper with a circulation of over 200,000 . . . except that all proper nouns (theater identification, film title, actors' names) have been replaced with charitable X marks. The reviewer makes his living writing reviews.

XXX presently is showing an outrageously funny film called "XXX." It has a deliciously antic script.

XX's direction has been fabulously witty and inventive. And a stellar cast turns in a performance it would be hard to match for wit, style and élan. Waste no time in seeing it.

The racy fable concerned with do's and don'ts for middle-aged gentlemen contemplating a gambol down the primrose path without disturbing wives or public images is not a romp for the unsophisticated or for prudes. Everyone else should have a chuckle-and-guffaw field day watching it.

XX never was more diverting than he is as the married man bent on having a fling. And XX has not had a happier casting than he has in the role of the raffish attorney who is the would-be rake's mentor. Comic genius in everything these two do.

No principal role is other than brilliantly polished off. As for the cameo bits allotted to the baker's dozen of guest stars, they all should have such juicy material to play around with in their feature films and television shows.

Brisk pace of the comedy is established in the action that backgrounds and points up the screen credits. As the madcap revel gets really going one instinctively braces himself for moments of letdown; and the possibility of an anticlimactic finale isn't discounted.

But there's never a letdown. As for the grand finale, a sound-track gag makes it a show-topper. If XXX gets its just deserts at the box office, it should be holding joyously forth for weeks to come.

Most people speak in conventional phrases, especially when the subject turns to the weather, sports and other everyday topics. But when a professional writer attempts to *describe* and *evaluate* a film, one hardly expects to receive an unending stream of stock phrases. Was the "review" composed by plugging the names of the characters and a few plot details into a ready-made template, rather like those

59

silly fill-in-the-blanks parlor games of the 1930s? Does the reviewer use a dartboard, a flip-book, a rotating file of adjectives, or some other mechanical device for assembling familiar phrases into what passes for a composition? Such cynicism is not unwarranted upon reading the above review.

To reveal the paucity of ideas, the utter lack of insight or fresh approach, one need merely tally the shopworn descriptive phrases:

outrageously funny	field day	brisk pace
deliciously antic	diverting	madcap revel
fabulously witty	happier casting	grand finale
stellar cast	comic genius	show-topper
racy fable	brilliantly polished off	just deserts
down the primrose path	juicy material	holding joyously forth

It should be said, though, that the film in question was a cliché-ridden comedy released across the country just in time for the summer movie season that depends more on air conditioning to bring 'em in than on stories with any substance. The film opened at the end of a hot week, and the reviewer may have been clearing his desk before taking off for three days at the lake cabin. At any rate, it was by far his sloppiest piece of the year.

Even on his bad days, a reviewer should recognize stale phrases that have been so overused that they fail to communicate. Saying that a play provides "a diverting evening" tells us nothing: so do power failures and contract bridge parties. A "diverting evening" tag line is a mere curlicue, an unimaginative way to dispose of the summarizing paragraph.

Similarly, to criticize a novelist for presenting "mere cardboard cutouts for characters" and leave it at that is to give the reader a mere cardboard cutout review. One test might be to ask of a sentence: Could this line be picked up and dropped into any of a dozen other reviews? If so, it lacks the specificity, the real information, that makes a review useful and valid.

Drama critics, running down the list of players and assigning appropriate adjectives, frequently tell us that so-and-so "provided a serviceable Willy Loman." The actor who—given a lead role in a classic—is judged merely "serviceable" must not have done a very good job. But we aren't sure. Serviceability can be construed to be a positive or a negative attribute. A critic uses the word to duck his responsibility for rating the performance. The reader who stops to ponder soon realizes he has been cheated: the adjective is completely hollow.

ADJECTIVES SHOULD DESCRIBE

The thoughtful reviewer is one who learns to distinguish between adjectives which merely *measure* or identify and adjectives which *describe* and illuminate. "Nice," "beautiful," "heartwarming" and "excellent" are words which categorize, but they leave us wondering: Nice in what way? Beautiful because of what qualities? Heartwarming to whom? Excellent by what standard? Another problem with superficial evaluative words is that they *tell* the reader instead of *showing* him. They impose an idea upon him instead of giving him the information he needs in order to form his own opinion. In the end, they insult intelligence.

In the following excerpts from effective reviews, notice how each writer eschews the obvious. A great deal of information is transported efficiently, and an image is drawn. The writer tries to make us *see* or *feel* what he saw and experienced:

Thomas Wolfe's great locomotives in the night ran over, but not through, Blake's country. Jack Kerouac went through here in a jalopy but stopped only at Dairy Queen stands. (Nelson Algren reviewing James Blake's *The Joint* in the *Los Angeles Times.*)

Mrs. Johnson comes across as a Bird in a gilded cage, worrying over her plumage and her offspring, making endless social rounds, beautifying her environment (without being able to strike at the sources of ugliness), pecking away at a mountain of correspondence. . . . (Christopher Lehmann-Haupt reviewing Lady Bird Johnson's *A White House Diary* in *The New York Times.*)

Matching the exquisite delicacy of her features, Claire Bloom moves with emotional assurance from the early phase of the wife as kept puppet to the later phase of the woman who issues an emancipation proclamation to her husband. The larky girlishness of the early Nora is always a bit of a problem, but Miss Bloom manages to be a trifle giddy without appearing inane. As the later Nora, her performance is informed with a grave clarity. (T. E. Kalem reviewing *A Doll's House* in *Time* magazine.)

REVIEWING FOR THE MASS MEDIA

On Broadway, the laughter is full, polite, airily uncommitted. At the American Place Theatre, the blacks in the audience stamp their feet and talk to the stage. The experience is speaking to part of their soul, and the white audiences—many for the first time—get intimations of their parochial feeling for the world. (John Lahr reviewing *Five on the Black Hand Side* in *The Village Voice*.)

In the two excerpts that follow, the writer assays the effectiveness of an acting job and a writing job, but not merely on scales of measurement. In both cases, *method* is analyzed so that the reasons for the surface appearance are clear.

Bedecked with spectacles and a walrus mustache that make him look like a latter-day Paul Muni and with the comedic approach of a Jewish Jack Lemmon, Segal gives an uneven performance too often lapsing into a sort of stultified reaction, never quite sure of how naive he is supposed to be. That his duets with Miss Streisand ultimately become monotonous shrieking bouts seems to be a fault of direction rather than performance. (Judith Crist reviewing *The Owl and the Pussycat* in *New York* magazine.)

The Great White Hope is one of those liberal, well-meaning, fervently uncontroversial works that pretend to tackle contemporary problems by finding analogies at a safe remove in history. In spite of Muhammad Ali, who was quoted two years ago as saying of the play, 'You just change the time, date and the details and it's about me!', Mr. Sackler's play and screenplay are too smug, too full of stereotypes to be provocative as drama. Similarly, his method is too pretentious to create the kind of fundamentalist fervor that might prompt one to interrupt the production by shouting an occasional 'Yes, Lord!' or 'Amen!' (Vincent Canby reviewing the film version of *The Great White Hope* in *The New York Times*.)

HALLMARK . . . OR RUT?

"That sounds just like Walter Kerr," the reader sighs—or moans, or smiles—as he sets down the Sunday arts and leisure section. Most critics with a regular platform eventually come to sound "just like" themselves. Judith Crist uses the word "banal" once a week, until it doesn't really mean banal anymore; it means "Judith Crist doesn't like this." Clive Barnes tosses the word "praise" around as if he were Santa with a bag full of praise to be passed out to the good kids. A midwestern drama critic discovered the word "modicum" lying around unused and quickly discovered a modicum of talent in a young actress, a modicum of taste in the set design of one production, a modicum of thought in the theme of another.

A reviewer ought to sit down with his clip book every few months and read over his latest outpouring of material. All at one sitting. If he detects faddish words or finds himself lolling in a phase, entertaining a passing fancy too long, he must jack himself up. Developing a style of writing is important in building a readership, but relying on a private vocabulary is not the way to go about it. Style is an extension of personality, not a by-product of word coinage or the thesaurus. Freshness and alertness are as important as anything; the writer who wants to do something specific to improve his style would do best to jog twice around the park, take a cold shower, and drink a glass of grapefruit juice.

8
Books:
Making Notes
on a Flyleaf

The lover of books has a special reverence for a volume newly pur-
chased at the bookstore or freshly stripped of gift wraps. If he has
acquired this devotion to the printed word under the aegis of a good
mother or a conscientious schoolteacher, he goes through a ritual
of first inspecting all the physical aspects of the object which includes
at least one thorough reading of the descriptive material, inside and
out. He places the spine of the book on a table, flattens the covers,
and proceeds to break in the binding, separating a few dozen pages
at a time from either end and running his finger along the seam.
When he has loosened the amalgam of gauze and glue sufficiently
to know in his bones that he has the feel of the book and the book
has the feel of him, he turns to the front. Not to Chapter One, but
to the stiff endpapers marked with the publisher's imprint, then to
the pages numbered "i" and "ii" and so on. He learns that the book
is in its second printing; the illustrations were supplied by the Bett-
mann Archives; portions of the text previously appeared in two obscure magazines; and the whole endeavor is dedicated to the loving
memory of the author's faithful companion of some fourteen years,
Bootsie, a cocker spaniel.

Most people who read are not lovers of books. Perhaps not even a majority of those who write reviews of books are given to minute inspections of the printer's and binder's handiwork. It makes little difference to the audience of a volume on indoor gardening that the text is set in Monticello, a Linotype revival of the original Binny & Ronaldson Roman No. 1, cut by Archibald Binny and cast in 1796 by a Philadelphia type foundry, although that information and more was offered by Alfred A. Knopf to purchasers of Thalassa Cruso's *Making Things Grow.* Unless a book is horrendously gotten up, of shoddy workmanship, and rife with typographical errors, there is not enough space in a book review to discuss such things as inks or margins.

Nonetheless, the book reviewer, to do his job honestly and competently, must get a genuine "feel" for the book, whether he runs his fingers down its seams or not. Before his eyes settle on the initial letter of the text, he must attempt to know what the book purports to be and what it promises to deliver. Once he begins to read, he measures it against that promise. And as he goes along he must observe which characteristics of the work are most telling and decide what few observations on his part will impart to his readers a comprehension of the book's worth.

DRAWING ON RESOURCE MATERIALS

Let us turn first to the reviewer's preparation for writing a book notice, beginning with the moment he receives a review copy from his editor. The book may come with inserts: a biography of the author, a handout notice consisting of a statement about the plot or a summary of a nonfiction book's content, and perhaps a last-minute item telling that the author has received an honor or that the book has just been accepted by a major book club.

In addition to looking over these tidbits and reading the promotional material on the dust jacket for biographical information, the reviewer should check to see whether the book is currently being excerpted in a magazine, or determine if parts of the book have previously appeared elsewhere. Increasingly, the book publishing business is dependent upon subsidiary publication in periodicals to create advance interest in titles. A novel by a major author is likely to be excerpted in *Esquire* or *McCalls,* and chapters from nonfiction books appear as much as a year before publication in any of hundreds of magazines. The reader whose appetite has been whetted will appreciate the note that portions of the book have previously appeared in another medium. A reviewer who lives in a vacuum runs the risk of embarrassment if he thinks he has uncovered a surprising statement in a book, only to be told by his editor that the item made news three months earlier when it was excerpted in *Life*.

Researching an author is not difficult; the dust jacket provides the basics, and previous books are usually listed on the back of the title page. Helpful reference books at the library include *Who's Who in America, Current Biography, Contemporary Authors* and *Book Digest*. Regular reviewers make a practice of reading various trade publications for advance information about new books and their authors. General magazines of intellectual appeal offer insight through interviews with authors of forthcoming books; the Trade Winds column of *Saturday Review* and the Talk of the Town column of *The New Yorker* are examples.

FAMILIARITY WITH THE AUTHOR

If the book is the second or third by an author, must the reviewer have read his earlier works? In the case of nonfiction, a highly qualified yes. Certainly anyone unfamiliar with the cult authors Hans Holzer and Edgar Cayce would be likely to commit gaucheries if he attempted to comment on the latest volumes of ESP or the supernatural to gush forth from their typewriters. Similarly, the witty works of C. Northcote Parkinson, beginning with *Parkinson's Law*, are cumulative in effect. The reviewer would be remiss if he ignored the current work's predecessors. Inevitably, the latest collaboration by Dick Schaap with a sports figure must be compared with or contrasted to the successful *Instant Replay*.

Other volumes may stand alone, although their authors may be prolific. Paul Gallico has written such a variety of books, ranging from the whimsical Mrs. 'Arris stories to wartime aviation adventures, that there is little profit in attempting to assess any one title in terms of his overall career.

In the case of novelists, the "yes" need not be qualified. The *vita* is virtually always of interest. Next to first love and first communion, the first novel is one of society's most revered institutions. First love may sour. Everybody sins before long. And most authors fall short of the Great American Novel. But the newcomer to the fiction fraternity is accorded the full rites of having his book reviewed as a *first novel*. The reviewer who fails to perform the ceremony is a heretic.

Supposing that a first novel is mildly successful—that is, that it sells at least 5,000 copies and collects a handful of good reviews—there will doubtless be a second novel. The critic who reviews it fails in his task if he has not read the first, because the literary world is waiting to know if a style is emerging, if the first book was a fluke or the beginning of a career. With the third and successive books, a following builds. The author's devotees are automatically the reviewer's most avid readers, so he should answer their first question: Is this one like the previous one?

Relating similar titles

The reviewer, guided by his editor, should also be aware of similar titles and should attempt to place the current book in a larger context. In the years since the Kennedy assassinations, there have been countless books on conspiracy theories and on the Kennedy family, ranging from William Manchester's serious *The Death of a President* to utterly irresponsible books centering on the Jim Garrison investigations in New Orleans. When yet another volume on the subject appears, it must be assigned its niche. The editor of a competent book review department makes certain that the book is assigned to someone who is familiar with the genre, and the reviewer in turn refreshes his memory by scanning his file of reviews before proceeding.

A growing practice—and a commendable one—in book review sections glutted by a backlog of new titles is the lumping together of books on similar subjects. *Saturday Review*, for example, assigned five related books (*Justice Denied: The Case for Reform of the Courts, Getting Justice: The Rights of People, With Justice for Some: An Indictment of the Young Advocates, Crime and Justice in American Society* and *The Rule of Law*), totaling 1,400 pages, to a social science professor who examined them in an essay entitled "Neglected Values Locked Into the Law." After an introductory section of more than 1,000 words, he turned to the five books, giving each about 250 words. Individual strengths and weaknesses were noted, and the reader was left to judge which volumes were of most use or interest to him.

No book exists in a vacuum—every work relates to others in some way. The reviewer of nonfiction should have one dominant question in his mind when he sets down a new title after reading it: How does this book serve the typical reader? A volume on mushrooms and toadstools, at first glance esoteric and apparently of interest only to botanists and naturalists, may relate to the general audience's growing concern with ecology, the environment and natural foods. *Men in Groups,* an examination of male bonding patterns ostensibly relevant only to anthropologists and sociologists, attracted much wider attention when early reviewers related the subject matter to the newly emerging Women's Liberation movement. The reviewer who has received the last choice of the new titles may, if he is alert and discerning, discover a hidden gem.

The reviewer of fiction, too, may be challenged by the most obscure and unassuming novel. Drawing upon the lifelong familiarity with literature which any reviewer should have, he, too, must ask one overriding question: Which of the classic themes does this story explore, and in what fresh ways? Half of the love stories written in the past four centuries are essentially the Romeo and Juliet tale told anew: *Abie's Irish Rose, West Side Story, Love Story* and so on. Even Shakespeare, whose plots are constantly being reworked in modern dress, dipped into history (usually English or Roman) and legend (usually Italian) for fresh material in order to meet the demands of his Elizabethan audiences.

Surprisingly, many reviewers don't take the long view; they fail to discern a book's thematic heritage or its literary niche. A study by Gerald Walker in *Writer's Yearbook* called attention to the myopia of American reviewers during the early 1960s. Walker, whose reviews have appeared in *The New York Times, The Village Voice, Saturday Review, Cosmopolitan* and other periodicals, was intrigued with the way in which a book called *The Stars in Their Courses* paralleled Homer's *Iliad.* Characters, action and even writing style were conscientiously matched by author Harry Brown to the classic mold. The book was, incidentally, a "Western" in that it was set in the old west. The publishers did not publicize the book's similarity to the *Iliad* in their advertisements or promotional pieces.

Walker examined 54 reviews from major newspapers and magazines across the country and found only 15 reviewers who recognized the derivation. The majority, including a few of the "biggies" on New York papers and magazines, failed to make any mention of it. Calling the reviewers who missed the thematic connection "clunks," Walker maintained that there is room in the ranks of American reviewers for more people whose "literary antennae" are sensitively tuned.

Another distressing study, this one at Wayne State University, showed that American book reviews tend to be overwhelmingly favorable or noncommittal—only a small percentage could be categorized as entirely unfavorable. Unfortunately, the typical reviewer, perhaps standing in awe of the completed book (as opposed to his own not-yet-begun effort), or perhaps not wanting to derail the gravy train that brings him free reading material, conceives of his task as either praising the book or going through the polite formalities of announcing its publication.

The American book publishing industry, which operates on a principle of flooding the market and letting the best sellers surface where they may, takes it for granted that most reviews will be at least favorable. Outright raves (augmented by trade gossip, late-night television appearances by "sexy" authors, and dumb luck) are necessary in order to push a book to the top of the so-called best-seller lists. They then "carry the list" for the publisher, giving his total publishing venture for the year a rosy profit picture. The entire publishing field might benefit in the long run if book reviewers across the nation took their machetes to the overgrown jungle of books and hacked away until only the hardiest specimens remained.

READING THE BOOK FOR REVIEW

Needless to say, a book must be read in its entirety before it is reviewed. ". . . And you'll have to read it yourself to find out" may be a satisfactory summing-up at a literary tea, but it won't suffice in any serious communication medium.

The project should be begun when the reader can give the work his undivided attention, and when he can be assured of completing the book within a reasonable time—no more than two or three days or evenings for the typical book. To permit distractions to interfere, or to drag out the task over a week or more, is a disservice to the author. Important details or plot turns at the beginning of the book may slip from mind if the reading is prolonged. The 500-word review attempts to give an accurate, fair "total impression" of the work, and that impression may be less than total if the book has been absorbed in parts instead of as a whole.

How to keep track of details? Some reviewers use standard, lined yellow legal pads for recording observations as they go along. Others use bookmark-sized strips of note paper, inserting one at each item— sometimes with cryptic notes written on the inch of paper that sticks out of the book. Reviewers who have no special reverence for the book may accomplish the same result by turning down the corners of key pages and underlining important passages.

The danger in any mark-as-you-go system is that the reviewer is likely to allow an initial impression to dominate his thinking and color his final analysis. Something that he finds on an early page puts a notion in his head—perhaps it even suggests an attack or a lead segment—and from then on he looks for additional bits of information that will support his first opinion. Some reviewers, fearing just that sort of prejudice, steadfastly refuse to take notes or mark passages. They let the total effect of the book cumulate naturally, preferring to search back through the text or to make a second "skim" reading in order to spot useful excerpts that support the opinion arrived at only after a full reading. Obviously, "knowing thyself" is important. Some reviewers prefer to monitor their reactions and tally them at the end; others feel they are most honest when they retrace their steps in order to document the original experience.

Variations in individual approaches are also found in the lapsed time between reading and writing. Turning to the typewriter immediately after completing the reading may enable one kind of writer— the journalist accustomed to working under deadline pressure, for example—to capture his feelings while they are fresh. An uncomplicated book, a story which has enthralled the reader, or a topic upon which the reviewer has strong feelings or considerable expertise may be well served by instant analysis. Conversely, a multileveled work, a story that creates a feeling of ambivalence in the reader, or a work that defies easy categorization may be better served by a period of "percolation" before the writing begins. Sleeping on a book, or even following it up with a reading of some related materials, may profitably lead to a more thoughtful review than is otherwise possible.

Some writers hate to lose a thought while it is banging around inside their cranium; they feel that the mental atoms approach "critical mass" soon after the outside matter is introduced. Other writers mistrust any notion that flashes across their mind too readily. They reason that, if a sudden vision is valid, it will endure as a lingering image. Again: know thyself.

After writing the review—whether quickly and with ease, or protractedly and with much soul searching—it is a good idea to put it away for a day. Coming back to it after rest or diversion, the writer usually finds that he is able to improve the piece through tightening to eliminate redundancies and by replacing inflated words with crisp, simple ones. It is also a good practice to verify each fact, spelling and textual citation one more time. The credibility of a critic evaporates quickly when simple, easily checked errors appear in his work, whatever the excuse.

ANALYZING THE BOOK REVIEW

In a later chapter we shall compare and contrast a selection of book reviews to see how various writers can approach one work. In the following pages we shall look at one complete book review and several excerpts for insight into the reviewer's methods of helping the reader to appreciate a new work.

Each week on page two of *Book World* Steven Kroll reviews four new novels, giving from 200 to 500 words to each book. Here is his notice for Jerzy Kosinski's *Being There*, a 142-page book published in the spring of 1971 by Harcourt, Brace, Jovanovich:

Being There is short. In fact *Being There* is so short it's almost not like being there at all. It's also very stylized, and in a small way rather devastating.

Chance—that's his name and his story—has always lived in the Old Man's house and tended the Old Man's garden. He has never been outside, never known his parents, never learned to read and write. He knows nothing but the garden—and TV. His non-personality is entirely the creation of the box, and 'by changing the channel he could change himself.' But the Old Man dies, and Chance is thrown into the street. Only to be struck immediately by a limousine.

Which is the beginning. Upset by her chauffeur's negligence, Mrs. Benjamin Rand, affectionately called EE, takes Chance home with her for medical attention. Home, and struggling for the right TV role, Chance offers a garden metaphor. The ailing, elderly Mr. Rand considers it profound. More such metaphors follow: for the president (who comes to visit the next day), for national television, for diplomats at the UN, for the news media and party guests. EE can't seduce him (because TV has never gone that far), but innocent, unreal Chance is an instant celebrity. Until rather too abruptly the novel swings full circle.

So we have a parable, a kind of perverse Horatio Alger story in a Ionesco mode. And Jerzy Kosinski is good at it—with his stripped-down prose, his sense of wit and irony, his knowledge of the careful programming of our assumptions. We have only a brief moment to weep before television and its non-people usurp our minds and hearts and bodies, and can we really say that even that moment remains?

Kosinski himself would probably doubt it. In his fiction there is no real human contact; life is always barren and devoid of energy. Only the imagery is sharp, precise, vivid, and it's the imagery you remember: the dark outlines of wartime horror in *The Painted Bird*, the somber little fragments of anomie in *Steps*, Chance's garden and TV soul. But the imagery conceals the author, who is always hovering close at hand yet always anonymous and cold. In praising Kosinski, let us hope he's not the person he has warned us against. (Reprinted by permission of *Book World*)

This is a compact review of a compact book. After a brief "teaser" paragraph, the review devotes exactly half its space to recounting the plot. The remainder discusses the author, his purpose, his style and his contribution.

Several elements of the review bear further analysis:

(1) The lead comments on the brevity of the work. Not that readers buy by the page, but some might just balk at paying $4.95 for such a slim novel. The reviewer comforts us with the knowledge that something good does come in this small package, although he is cryptic enough to keep our interest up. "Rather devastating" plays a wishy-washy modifier against a potent adjective. The result of that ploy is to give the reader an index early in the review, at the same time hedging because of necessary qualifications.

(2) To summarize plot, or not: that is the question in reviewing every novel. Here the reviewer gives us the bare bones, and he manages to be appropriately enigmatic at the crucial points: we are not told what the "garden metaphors" are, nor do we get an explanation of how the novel "swings full circle." The frequent lone phrases and short sentences serve various purposes: they acknowledge the absurdity of the plot (we get the impression that the story is *supposed* to be as absurd as it sounds), they make it clear that the reader is

being given an especially truncated version of the story, and finally they reflect the style of the book itself to some extent.

(3) Although a temptation exists to insert observations, comments and sometimes loaded adjectives about the plot line, the reviewer has avoided it. He appears to have attempted to present the story as objectively as possible. Only in the last line of the two paragraphs of plot summary is the reader told that the novel swings full circle "rather too abruptly." In this position it acts as a transition from fact to opinion; in the next paragraph the judgment begins.

(4) The final paragraphs do a variety of things quite nicely. The book is categorized in terms of other writers' works. It is placed in context with the author's two previous novels. In the middle of each of the paragraphs, Kosinski's writing style is described—both times in terms of its spare, sharp-edged qualities, partially answering the questions raised by the lead.

(5) Both of the final two paragraphs pose questions: Is it too late to save ourselves? Is the author the threat? By moving the reader front and center (he is being talked about; he may be the victim) and by posing the questions, the reviewer gives the reader the ultimate task of judging for himself. In effect, then, this is a "positive" review, because the reviewer is telling us to read the book. But with the recommendation comes a seed of doubt.

Is the review a "cop-out" in that it remains enigmatic? We may safely say no on several grounds. First, enough material is presented to indicate that the book is of interest only to the reader who has enough intelligence to work along with a "perverse parable." We may safely assume that such a person does not require a cut-and-dried summary. Second, upon reading the reviewer's other pieces on the same page, we ascertain that he is quite capable of summarizing precisely and unequivocally, should he feel that it is warranted. And finally, if we have heard Kosinski speak (he made several campus and television appearances in the weeks following publication), we know that the man leaves very much the same impression in person that he does in print, and that the reviewer has captured the essence of it here.

SOME ENDINGS: 75-25 AND 25-75

Typically, after sketching a plot and weighing the merits of the author's approach to a theme, the reviewer tries to subtotal and total up his feelings in a summary paragraph. Occasionally his ambivalence manifests itself in what could be called a 50-50 judgment. Typically, however, the writer finds himself striving to tie it all together neatly so that his last words, if converted to a raw score, yield a 75-25 or a 25-75. That is, he likes the book, but with certain reservations; or, conversely, he finds he must reject the book's general premise, while conceding certain appeal.

Los Angeles Times reviewer John Weisman accorded a 75-25 verdict to Rex Reed's *Big Screen, Little Screen.* Early in his essay he discussed Reed's weak credentials as an academic critic: ". . . Reed sometimes stands on precariously thin aesthetic ice." As he proceeds to discuss the author's writing, he criticizes the flashy journalistic style and the intrusion of ego. Once those peccadilloes are disposed of, the reviewer finds much to praise. His final stanza is a perfect example of the 75-25:

> Perhaps the best thing about Rex Reed's reviewing is that it is highly stylized. It doesn't have the depth of, say, a Stanley Kauffmann or a Manny Farber, but it has a kind of *sprezzatura* all its own; a performer's shiny flair that, because it is entertaining, often more than compensates for its aesthetic misdirections. *Big Screen, Little Screen* is a glossy hunk of Tinsel Town, put together by one of show biz's best package wrappers.

Rex Reed might not see 75-percent gold in that piece of ore if he underlined the phrases he'd just as soon rewrite. But the tone is so breezy and complimentary overall that the carping points are definitely outweighed. The message appears to be: Sure, go right out and buy the book.

A review of *The Paragon,* a novel by John Knowles, for the *Miami Herald* exemplifies the reverse thrust: 25-75. Reviewer Paul Janaro, author of a writing text, begins his piece with a remark that "it is impossible to be altogether negative" about the book because it is "too cinematically written not to hold your interest." He then quickly attributes this to "an obvious eye on an immediate Hollywood sale," which tends to negate whatever compliment there was in the opening lines.

After discussing the story of an alienated young man on a campus in less complicated times, he moves to his 25-75 conclusion:

> I doubt that *The Paragon* holds much for Lou Colfax's present-day Ivy League counterparts. Knowles simply doesn't cope with the con-

sciousness that eventually blows up the geology lab, but he rather frustratingly makes us think about such things by writing so entertaining a novel and then failing to relate it to our troubled times. Some older readers will, however, enjoy it for nostalgic reasons, and not a few may welcome a fairly old-fashioned, literate, and relatively innocent change of fare from a steady diet of drugs and sex.

This version of the 25-75 summary echoes the frequent closing comment of the drama critic: It is likely to find an audience. One might surmise that the principal reason for hedging a bit is that the majority of books do find an audience, however small or specialized. Thus it would be presumptuous to label the book of no interest. The problem in this type of closing remark is that it tends to be condescending toward the eventual readers: in this case, it has been strongly suggested that they are escapists, or worse, old fuddy-duddies.

A thorny issue raised by the review which says "the author failed to relate his story to present-day realities" is this: does the reviewer have the right to question the issue of when and where a story is set, to whom and of what its author chooses to speak? Must all fiction have contemporary relevance? Here the reviewer believes so, and it is the basis for his serious reservation about the worth of the book. But it is not always a reasonable demand; it draws much too rigid parameters for the novelist: "You must speak to us in a way that relates to our current concerns." The edict, if strictly observed, might rule out many of our classics which exist only to show us how a certain person responded to his situation at a certain remote time. Many a reader would prefer to draw his own modern parallels rather than be convinced by the author that the theme or the circumstances are "relevant." One might even argue that the demands for relevance reflect a current shortsighted and thoroughly spoiled attitude among those who want "immediate payoff," instant gratification. "We must grant the artist his subject, his idea, his donnée," said Henry James in *The Art of Fiction.* "Our criticism is applied only to what he makes of it."

All this is by way of spotlighting a recurring problem in reviewing, not necessarily to criticize Janaro for his dismissal of the Knowles book. A reader would have to decide for himself whether the criticism was justified. Hence the 25-75 summary: the reviewer rightfully leaves the final decision to the reader.

CAREERS IN PROGRESS

Earlier we acknowledged the importance of reviewing the "first novel" and subsequent early works. Another familiar category with which the reviewer frequently finds himself dealing is the work of a well-established—and perhaps prolific—author. It was a rare Thanksgiving Day when John O'Hara failed to unveil his latest effort; indeed, each major American publisher has two or three "important" authors who produce steadily, bringing in a new book at regular intervals of two or three years.

The obvious questions on the reader's, and thus the reviewer's, mind are: Is the author in familiar territory or new? Is he up to his usual effort, or even better, or are signs of staleness evident? Is there a legitimate reason for this book (for the author's writing it, for our buying and reading it) or does it seem to have been produced merely because another book seemed due from the author?

The reviewer is placed in an awkward position when he confronts the latest effort from an author who appears to be bent upon producing the legendary five-foot shelf. If he praises, he may feel like a mere courtesan privileged to cry Hail! in the presence of the reigning king. Thus there is a temptation to be the one who dares prick the bubble, dismissing the work of an established author and predicting the beginning of his decline as well. Or there is a safe way out: a reviewer may restrict his work to criticizing unknowns and let other reviewers dash themselves to pieces wrestling with the literary gods.

In a relatively short period *The New York Times* daily book review column delivered blows to the reputations of three American literary giants:

Christopher Lehmann-Haupt said of Leon Uris's latest: "It is so undemanding. One can read it while engaged in activities that demand less than one's complete attention—activities like skywriting or climbing the Matterhorn . . . it acts as a kind of ballast to mental activity . . . you can do anything you like while reading it. In fact, you needn't even bother to read it at all."

Walter Clemons said of Philip Wylie's latest: "What can I tell you? I'd rather not review this thing at all. Stuck with it, the easiest out is 'Good old Philip Wylie, he sure can dish it out!' Still in there slugging. Praise the vigor of his scatter-gun vituperation. But, you know, he really isn't much good."

Anatole Broyard on Mary McCarthy's latest: "There are some bludgeoning attacks on 'American types' that are astonishing coming from a writer of Miss McCarthy's talent and sophistication. Where she was once ironical about her country and its people, she now seems merely exasperated—an exasperation with an edge of hysteria in it . . . they're not making boys the way they used to. And Miss McCarthy isn't writing books the way she used to, either."

The preceding excerpts are harsh, and they accurately reflect the overall tone of the complete reviews. The complaints were adequately explained, with references to the plot and to the writing style of the author in question.

One thread of similarity ran through the three reviews, as well as others published during the same season: the younger critics consistently upbraided the older writers for their views of America today. Wylie and McCarthy, especially, were criticized for crotchety passages detailing their disgust with the American scene and for inflexible attitudes toward the young. Any one of these and similar reviews would be merely interesting, but taken together they provide an emerging picture of a generation of readers out of tune with a generation of writers. It is an important development.

When an established author exceeds his previous efforts, the reviewer may be hard put to indicate that plaudits must now be converted to out-and-out raves. Novelist-essayist Benjamin DeMott managed it in his *Saturday Review* discussion of Norman Mailer's *Of a Fire on the Moon:*

> The plain case is, indeed, that Norman Mailer's account of Apollo 11 stands (despite a thousand defects) as a stunning image of human energy and purposefulness, and drives the audiences to regions of vibrant fact hitherto unimagined in writing. At those moments when the work rises to the level of its highest aspirations, it is itself an act of revelation—the only verbal deed to this moment that begins to be worthy of the drama and the reality it celebrates.

Wow! as Mailer himself would not say. This is the kind of critical comment he was obviously dreaming of when, in frustration over the coolness accorded him by reviewers, Mailer assembled examples of his early writing in a book aptly titled *Advertisements for Myself.*

When *The Prisoner of Sex* brought predictably harsh reviews from feminist critics, Mailer could get out his *Moon* clips for assurance that he was on top as an author.

THE REVIEWER AS A (FIRST) PERSON

As we saw earlier, one issue that is constantly surfacing in discussions of review techniques is the use of the first person singular. In each area of culture there are various arguments for and against the practice. In book reviewing, the pro arguments probably outweigh the con. Books are consumed on a one-to-one basis: one reader at a time. The act of reading a book is one of the most personal cultural experiences, so the reaction is one of the most personal, too. Read a collection of opera reviews and you rarely encounter an "I." But turn to the book page and it is common. As discussed earlier, critics of music and the theater automatically cover all performances falling in their purview, while book reviewers select or are selected—they are purposely matched to the books they review.

It is not uncommon, then, to find a reviewer discussing *his* camp counsellor days or *his* pet dog before reviewing a book on summer adventure or a volume on canine care. He establishes his credentials, his interest in the topic or his reason for finding something intensely likable or dislikable about the book. Part of the "I" phenomenon in book reviewing may also be attributed to the notion that the reviewer has a strong sense of "communicating" with the author—McLuhan would explain it as typical linear response. The reviewer has just finished following, word by word, line by line, the communication of an author, and now he has the opportunity to draft his reply. Whereas the drama critic is thinking of the potential audience when he writes his piece, the book reviewer is just as likely to be thinking of the author. He introduces himself accordingly.

Sometimes the reviewer knows the author or the subject of the book. "Dear Bob Dylan: You remember me . . ." one writer began his review of *Tarantula*. Structured to resemble a letter, the essay recounted the time the author congratulated the folk singer after a concert. The review was, in effect, a fan letter follow-up to this fleeting live contact of years before.

John Kenneth Galbraith, the economist, started his review of *My Years in Public Life* by Chester Bowles this way: "Truth, not unconvincing humility, is the grandest virtue and accordingly I may observe that I am better qualified than any man alive to review a book on the public life of Chester Bowles."

It is even possible for the reviewer to refer to himself in the third person: "A stupor had come over the book reviewer. He was numb . . ." Definitely Maileresque. And most editors allow it only once in a great while.

9
Drama:
Making Notes
on a Playbill

The American theater is escaping.

It hasn't fled across the border or disappeared from sight. On the contrary, it's escaping *to* us, not from us. After a century of confinement in a tiny box called the proscenium stage, it has thrust its way into our midst once more. After a century under house arrest between 42nd and 54th Streets, it has taken off through the fields, over the mountains and into the valleys across the land. Hallelujah!

The theater is even escaping the domination of the critics. In his book *Thirty Plays Hath November*, Walter Kerr noted that, because of the reduced number of critics and the rise of the preview system, the "power" over plays is shifting away from the critics toward the audiences. Kerr lauds the development, insisting that the remaining critics are interested in persuasion, not power: "They want to be part of a conversation, not a catastrophe."

Two events of the 1960s represented turning points in the American theater. Neither was set in motion by members of the Broadway establishment.

At the beginning of the decade, British producer-director Tyrone Guthrie selected Minneapolis as the location for a new repertory theater that eventually came to bear his name. He based his choice on several factors. The Twin Cities and their suburbs were clearly hungry for culture. The area already supported a first-rate symphony orchestra, a chamber orchestra, modest opera and ballet companies, and two or three excellent art museums. The civic leaders were willing to go "big league" in all respects, having just landed major baseball and football franchises. The main campus of the University of Minnesota had a thriving theater program and was eager to participate in workshops and experimental productions with a professional group. And perhaps as important as anything, Broadway was 1,253 miles to the east, too far to exert much influence.

Events occurred in Minnesota that just weren't happening along Broadway. *Hamlet* took on a new dimension, performed in modern dress. A new translation of *The House of Atreus* was performed in stunning masks. A breathtaking stage facility placed the action at the center of the audience, the audience at the center of the action. Theatergoers filled the tiers of multicolored seats for every production, not just those that drew unanimous raves. Good tickets sold for four and five dollars, and they were available. Instead of an intermission bell, a jubilant trio of trumpeters sounded the call from balconies in the lobby. A new theater was made, and a new audience was made for it.

Near the end of the decade, a young producer named Michael Butler hired an off-Broadway director named Tom O'Horgan to stage the rock musical *Hair* in a legitimate Broadway house. O'Horgan, whose previous directing experience included avant-garde productions at Greenwich Village's Cafe La Mama, was given the Biltmore Theater to work with—a standard house with a place for the actors to work and a place for patrons to sit and watch. But he didn't allow a demarcation line to exist; the footlights were put away. There was also some question about where the back of the stage was supposed to be, when exactly the play started and who exactly was in the play. A group of street people wandered in and a loosely related series of events transpired, many of them musical. While the audience members really didn't participate, neither were they permitted to merely watch. They were made to feel part of what was happening. Later, across the street where *Lenny* was playing at the Brooks Atkinson Theater, O'Horgan would create a situation whereby the play could not begin until the audience generated the action through a rhythmic clapping game. Night after night, audiences willingly helped get things rolling instead of sitting dumbly and waiting for 800 pounds of maroon velvet to rise and reveal a story in progress.

Fortunately, the Twin Cities are not the only towns with a burgeoning theater enterprise, and Tom O'Horgan is not the only director to invite the audience aboard a roller coaster. By the beginning of the 1970s, the theater was showing signs of a revitalization outside the dominion of Broadway, and that means that critics will be busy in Atlanta, Dallas, Los Angeles and Washington and on dozens of college campuses where the American Playwrights Theatre is taking new plays for original production.

The APT was formed by successful playwrights who believe that the way to build a healthy national theater is to let a new work find its voice among many audiences across the country. Consequently, the writers are offering some of their plays first to small theater groups. One Robert Anderson play, for example, received its premiere under the Ohio State football stadium, where a summer town-and-gown theater series is staged.

Taking the bad with the good

All of the preceding enthusiasm and encouragement for the drama criticism picture is by way of balancing some of the bitter indictments aimed at both the Broadway theater and its judges in recent years. Emory Lewis leveled a particularly stinging blow at the theater, its critics and its audience in his book *Stages: The Fifty-Year Childhood of the American Theater:*

> Selling shopworn goods which its brainwashed and culturally disadvantaged audiences do not seriously question, Broadway all too accurately reflects the sick society outside its doors. It is a truism that America and Broadway deserve each other. Broadway also gets, more often than not, the kind of critics it deserves. These gentlemen, in the main, mirror the prejudices, desires, and goals of the public. Judging the feckless fare of Broadway is hardly a satisfactory occupation for a man of sense and sensibility, unless he has fallen into masochistic habits. Few men of stature express interest in the practice of drama criticism. More and more it has become a job a man has every right to be ashamed of.

If that were all Lewis had to say—if he favored closing down Broadway and forcing all critics into a different line of work—a rebuttal would be in order. But he goes on to argue for better critics and better theater. The critics are killing the theater with kindness, he believes. Lewis calls for critics who dare to "blast away at the very foundations of our dangerously corrupt society as well as our rotting theater." He attacks today's critics for not keeping up with ballet, opera, music and art, as well as "global politics and commitment."

Lewis's remarks are as blunt as any since George Bernard Shaw wrote in the preface to his play *Saint Joan:* "To a professional critic (I have been one myself) theater-going is the curse of Adam. The play is the evil he is paid to endure in the sweat of his brow; and the sooner it is over the better."

Certainly professional drama reviewing leads to a different view of the theater from the one familiar to "hit" audiences. The "hit" playgoer sees only the shows which received unanimous reviews, or which were recommended to him by friends with similar tastes. So he sees mostly plays he enjoys; the theater for him is a dependable, pleasurable experience—one he can build an evening of drinks and supper around. William Goldman, in his excellent chronicle of a theater year, *The Season,* laments this "eventness" of attending a Broadway show.

But the critic, who must attend *all* the plays, sees a theater that includes occasional ineptness and a great number of not-too-near misses. He knows that it is easiest to write a rave notice—happy adjectives leap quickly to mind. But more often he will have to struggle to explain a play's apparent purpose, where it failed its goal, and what rewards remain to be found. He knows the theater's batting average well enough not to be surprised when he finds himself composing a review that damns with faint praise. That most critics still *like* the theater after sitting through so many weak and hopeless opened-closed-same-night plays is testimony to their fortitude and dedication. What makes it worthwhile, of course, is the occasional evening in the theater when the mind is engaged, the imagination is stretched, the intellect is rewarded. Or the glittering, happy finale of a new musical that gives us a story as well as songs which will live a long time. On these rare occasions, the critic is exhilarated, happy to be the messenger bearing good tidings.

PREPARING TO REVIEW THE PLAY

Doing homework on a play differs from preparing to review a book. There is always time to put a book aside and check various references, perhaps even reread a previous work by the same author. The relative leisureliness of book reviewing permits thorough checking and pondering at any point in the process.

The theater, however, happens in a few short hours, at an appointed time, and the review is usually due on the editor's desk an hour or so afterwards. Thus all preparation must be done ahead; it is of no use to sit and wish during the second act that you had taken the time to read up on the subject.

Here are some examples of how various critics prepared to view certain plays:

An Outer Circle reviewer seeing a light comedy admitted that he rarely prepares for reviewing. "I certainly wouldn't bother to prepare for a comedy. I know whether it's funny, whether it would appeal to the readers. My own spontaneous reaction is good enough. If it turned out to have a double meaning, a serious side, I doubt that I'd miss it or feel suddenly unequipped to handle it. Or if it appeared to be a retread of some earlier play or theme, I'm sure I'd recognize it . . . I've been going to the theater for twenty years. That's preparation for just about everything except a forgotten classic."

A campus reviewer assigned to see young playwright Sam Shepard's *Sidewinder* at the Lincoln Repertory remembered reading the play a few years earlier in *Esquire* magazine. Rereading it proved helpful, but the reviewer stopped after the first act, leaving the second act unread so that it would be fresh upon viewing. "That way I freed myself to really sit back and judge the acting and the staging in the first act. As it turned out, my review was mostly about the message of the play—what Shepard was getting at. Of course I had seen one of his one-acters Off-Broadway, so I knew what to expect."

A reviewer preparing to view an "updated" Shakespearean comedy (modernized with a biracial cast and rock lyrics) took the Bard's *Complete Works* from the shelf for the first time since college days and read not only the play but even the anthologist's discussion of Shakespearean comedy and the themes of the play. "I must have seen a hundred performances of Shakespeare's plays since college, but dipping into the book reminded me of some of the liberties they took in the Elizabethan theater. Remembering that, I felt more secure when I said in my review that the 'tampering' with lines and characters was interesting and justified."

One critic steadfastly refused to do any preparation for a Pinter play he had not previously seen. "I usually go to the library and look up the London reviews of British imports. Sometimes you have to judge why a play succeeded over there and bombed over here. But Pinter is something else. The more you read what people have said about his latest play, the more you start playing games. Everybody knows Pinter is enigmatic. Why prepare for enigma? I just eat lightly, so I won't fall asleep, and go to the theater. My review tells the reader what happened in the theater."

A weekly newspaper reviewer makes a habit of clipping the advertisement or show poster and checking over all the names in the production. "I'm a theater buff myself, and I think a lot of people like to know that someone who was in another play they liked is also in this one. That's especially so in local or summer theater; a lot of minor players have a following. I usually work the mention into my review if I can."

Should the reviewer read the play before seeing it? It's not usually possible with new plays, but it is with classics and revivals. On college campuses, where classics are the staple of the teaching theater, the reviewer probably will choose to read the script. There are two good reasons for it. First, a number of his readers will have thus prepared themselves, so the burden is also on the critic. Where the audience works harder, so must the reviewer. And, second, in a teaching theater the emphasis of the director-professor is often upon literal interpretation and classic production. His students are attempting to "do" Shakespeare or Ibsen or Molière. In order to judge the result, the reviewer needs to have the standard.

Clive Barnes of *The New York Times* did a rather curious thing in a recent season when he reviewed the Archibald MacLeish adaptation of Stephen Vincent Benét's *The Devil and Daniel Webster,* brought to Broadway as *Scratch.* Early in his review he wrote: "I cannot recall the short story with absolute clarity, but it seems to me that Mr. MacLeish has opened out its slender anecdotal fabric to admit broader issues concerned with a man's conscience and his belief in America." Later in the same piece he wrote: "The writing of the play—and I have read it and seen it twice—seems complacently mediocre."

It seems a bit strange that the critic has read the play and seen it twice, yet he has not made even a quick, easy reference to the original story, which is included in almost every major anthology of American literature. (Here we are getting frightfully close to the oft-heard charge that Barnes, a Britisher, has a subtle anti-American bias.) But at least we must agree that the critic is completely open and scrupulous regarding his preparation: at every turn he makes it quite clear exactly what is the extent of his familiarity.

Most critics prefer not to read scripts even when they are available to them. Most plays are not meant to be read, they are meant to be performed. Even if one has sufficient theatrical acumen to read a script intelligently, he is likely to create an interpretation in the mind that differs from what the director seeks. The critic wanders too far from his post in the audience when he overprepares to the point where he "sees" the play from a vantage point in the wings.

Most critics, if they do any advance reading at all, are attempting to equip themselves to discuss the theme of the play or the continuing theme of the author. In other words, they read *about* the playwright's previous works, or they read another author's work that covers similar territory. Whether or not the other works are mentioned in the review, the writer comes to the theater feeling better prepared to deal with the play's concept.

FLASHLIGHTS AND OTHER EQUIPMENT

Before the gold fringe of the curtain touches the dusty stage floor, most of the critics are half way up the aisle. Any usherette foolish enough to stand in the doorway at the rear of the house is bound to be bowled over in the rush. Interestingly enough, this urge to stampede is so ingrained in critics that they do it even when attending matinees, or when their papers are on strike. Critics just don't know how to leave a theater except by rocket.

To their credit, however, most critics arrive quietly and unobtrusively, often because they are required to pick up their complimentary tickets fifteen minutes before the curtain. Some of them don't want to acknowledge one another's presence for fear of setting off rumors about a critics' conspiracy against the play. So they hunch down in their seats and study the program.

Not the least of the reasons for reading the entire program carefully is to find any notes by the director concerning what he is trying to do. It's also a good idea to read the capsule career biographies of the leads. The reviewer who says "I think the director was striving for a dual effect . . ." or "If memory serves me, Miss Jones has

86

played this role before . . ." may be deluged with letters from play-goers who read facts to the contrary in the program. He may soon lose his editor's confidence as well as his readers'.

At the same time, it must be remembered that programs are not infallible sources of information. They are assembled by producers who willingly dress up the facts to suit their own publicity purposes. And the information comes from people who have a habit of remembering the good and forgetting the bad. In recent years the hip young theater people have taken to creating exotic and entirely fictitious pasts for themselves, frequently alluding to their royal blood and their international escapades.

The main reason for absorbing the program in the minutes before the curtain rises is to become familiar with the cast's names and roles so that they can be called up without the use of a flashlight. About the only writing most critics are able to do in the darkness of a performance is a few cryptic notes about those players who have been most or least effective. An apt adjective that suggests itself during an entrance or a reaction to an important speech might be forgotten before the final curtain.

In general, though, the critic does little writing in the dark or by the beam of a penlight. It is far more important to arrive at a general truth, a summarization of the principal strength or weakness of the play. Once the approach to the essay is arrived at—it may happen midway through the first act, or not until the curtain falls, or maybe not even until the paper is in the typewriter—then the other elements arrange themselves in relation to that theme. There is probably only enough space for one or two comments about each element of the production, so that copious notes are hardly necessary.

INTERMISSIONS, PRO AND CON

Drama critics are at odds over intermissions. A number of them have written reviews and columns criticizing intermissionless plays such as *1776* and *Man of La Mancha*. The complaints center around either the inability of the audience to sit still for over two hours or the advantages of giving the playgoers an opportunity to discuss the play at its midpoint. The latter is especially crucial in mystery plays, serious drama and plays in which the passage of time is supposed to occur during the break in action.

Critics who endorse plays without intermissions say they prefer the action to be unbroken. They are just as happy to forgo the choking smoke, the wretched orange drinks and the prattle that characterize most theater foyers at the halfway point.

A few reviewers use the intermission to draft a potential lead paragraph on the back of the program. If nothing else, when the play is over and they begin to write, it provides a good reminder of what their attitude was halfway through the evening. It can also help them organize their minds and eyes so they can look for telling points in the final act which will support and illustrate their premise.

ANALYZING THE NEW PLAY

Because there are different problems inherent in the reviewing of a new play as opposed to a revival, we shall look at two reviews by critic Ernest Albrecht of the New Brunswick, N. J., *Home News*. First, the new play:

Elliott Caplin is obviously an intelligent person. Unfortunately nobody has ever been able to prove that intelligence is really a prerequisite for being a playwright. Much more important is a sense of the dramatic, an understanding of the theater. Without these qualities Caplin's play 'Any Resemblance to Persons Living or Dead . . .' is merely an intelligent discussion of the sources of power. It lacks sustaining interest, humor (despite its being billed as a comedy), and dramatic energy.

Caplin's narrative deals with a young man determined to be an earth-shaker. He understands that power is won and manipulated through money, politics and religion. The obstacles to be surmounted are the intelligentsia and militant minorities.

One by one, without struggle and with very little effort, he achieves financial, political and religious power. The money he gets by inventing a polyethylene woman who can do anything a real woman can do except demand anything in return. The other two power bases are acquired so easily that I cannot quite relate the actual means.

The earth-shaker-to-be merely does a lot of quick talking, fiddles with a few gadgets, shoots a few people who might stand in the way—and we are to accept the fact that he has replaced God and Nixon (in that order).

The complete absence of any sort of struggle robs the play of the surface tension needed to hold it together. Nor is it very clear what the young man is up to exactly, so that aside from trying to figure out how he has managed his latest trick, we may also be set to wondering why he bothered.

Caplin's understanding of the world's brain trust is perhaps the most interesting aspect of the play. 'Put them up to their armpits in research grants so that they'll never have to earn a cent.' Otherwise, although his understanding of the sources of power is complete, there is nothing particularly unique in his observations, and what is worse they are presented as if they were some obscure truths suddenly being revealed. But even if that were the case, the playwright must find some way of making his statement in terms of the theater.

In place of a dramatic text, Loukas Skipitaris has directed his cast in all manner of extravagant overacting—believing, perhaps, that the phony theatrics of ham acting would hide or replace the playwright's failure to use the theater.

Ruth Warrick is the most desperate example of this. She poses vocally and physically, placing herself and her words onto one pedestal after another. Rather than being appealingly ruthless and wise, she comes off merely as an actress who hasn't been in the theater for a long time and thinks the stage calls for the grand manner.

John Call, as the ex-richest man in the world, and Tex Thurston, as a political cliché, indulge in a farcical style, but I am inclined to believe that is because of the director's faith in the show as a comedy.

Matthew Tobin, as an old professor, almost manages to make some dramatic sense and comedy out of the character's contradictory values. He is both senile and brilliant. It's a struggle that must necessarily invite certain indulgences, but I am tempted to forgive Tobin, because he is the most fun the play ever generates.

Marc Alaimo, as the central character, is trapped with a collection of diabolical stances that swing between the pretentious and the melodramatic. At least, he never looks downright absurd.

'Any Resemblance, etc.' bears very little resemblance, therefore, to a play. It never engages us to a point where we really care to sort out its confused simplicity or apply its generalizations to any more interesting specific.

When approaching a new work, the first question in the reviewer's mind is, simply enough: Is there a play here? Often the answer is no. If the answer is no, it is possible to ask a more generous version of the question: Is what happens on the stage truly *theater*, or is it merely a message that belongs in another medium? *The Great White Hope* was written in verse, *The Trial of the Catonsville Nine* is a literal court record, *Story Theater* is the playacting of children's fairy tales. Yet all are theater, all are drama.

Albrecht is not being cruel or unfair when he focuses on the author's intelligence and ability in his lead paragraph. He has put his finger on the problem, and he feels there is a lesson in it for reader and playwright alike.

The second, third and fourth paragraphs detail the plot—enough to give the reader a fair idea of what the play is about, but not so much as to give the entire story away. The synopsis is plain and unadorned, but word choices and sentence structure (both very casual) give the reader to understand that the reviewer finds the plot rather too facile and cute.

Having done that, the reviewer returns in the fifth and sixth paragraphs to the point raised in his lead. Now, because the reader knows the outline of the story, the writer is able to elaborate his contention that the play lacks the necessary elements of good theater.

The next five paragraphs cite the director and each of the leading players. This section is standard, of course, except in plays in which ensemble performance overshadows individual contribution, or in instances in which some overriding issue takes so much space that there is no place for individual mentions. If the reader is told more than he needs to know here about each principal role, perhaps it is the result of a lack of interest in the play itself. Albrecht takes care to place some of the burden for the actors' performances on the director. Having acted and directed himself, he is well equipped to pinpoint the cause.

The final paragraph returns to the theme of the lead, and it offers a totaled-up scorecard. Albrecht's opinion was closely in line with other media critics'; the play closed after nine performances.

Some of Albrecht's sentences and paragraphs are long, perhaps approaching the limit of reading ease and comprehension. But the all-important opening and closing paragraphs are crisp. And each of the four sections of the review is introduced by a terse statement which is supported and explained in the ensuing sentences.

ANALYZING SUBSEQUENT PRODUCTIONS

Now let us turn to another of Albrecht's reviews, one that looks at a production of a Broadway hit from an earlier season.

When 'Child's Play' opened in New York a few seasons ago, it was hailed as a spellbinding new play. It had its problems even then, an ending that is forced and unsatisfactory, but seeing it again at Bucks County one is struck by the fragility of the play and the enormously important contribution made by the acting, directing and scene design in New York that kept it from falling completely apart. With each of these elements reduced in New Hope, the play seems ordinary, listless and overrated.

The performances of Dana Andrews and Robert Coucill as the protagonists in the current production are in all respects adequate, mild portrayals of recognizable schoolteacher types. But if the play is to have any great effect, the two men must be more than just recognizable. They transcend their ordinariness with mysticism and mystery.

Instead of clichés of pedagogues, the stars in New York suggested two demons whose powers one could never quite grasp but were felt with a chilling, uneasy surety. Their strengths and weaknesses coalesced into an all-pervading fear. Andrews and Coucill are able to project none of these mysterious qualities. They are wholly ordinary, making the play's extraordinary events too easy to dismiss as merely farfetched.

The problem of the ending is that the playwright, Robert Morasco, tries to give a rational explanation to the irrational behavior. It simply won't go down. When the performances reduce the play entirely to a level of ordinariness in the production, we are . . . always suspicious of it. It is difficult to believe that these people have anything to do with the evil around them, which now seems wholly gratuitous and therefore less than frightening.

The original direction, in a setting that was dark and brooding, suggesting twisted subterranean depths and foreboding upper reaches, sent the violence through the play like a cold shiver. The bloody cruelty taking place in this Catholic boys' school was caught only in glimpses. It was gone with a quiver, almost as if it hadn't been there.

Lee R. Yopp's direction lingers a bit longer over these moments, perhaps in the mistaken idea that he could make the play's horror more palpable by letting us see more of it. The reverse is true. The unknown horror, the instinctively felt but unseen, is far more frightening than anything we can actually see.

The setting here, pushing the Bucks County stage to its limits, has definite beginnings and endings and is too distinctly lighted, allowing us to make too many judgments and delineations that the play cannot really tolerate. We can see where people come from and go. They do not slip in and out as phantoms. Yopp's direction in such a setting serves to make the action too substantial.

The supporting cast, for the most part, projects consistent fear when uneasiness would be more to the point of unsettling us.

Fear is too real and heavy to be easily transferred to an audience, particularly when we have so ample an opportunity to assess its source and find it unnecessary. We are never able to feel the fear written in all the furrowed brows and frozen features.

Jittery uneasiness we could have participated in if the production had not insisted on being throughout as plausible as its author insists it is at the end. A twilight zone rationale would have been far more stimulating than all the dreary realistic melodrama we are asked to believe in at Bucks County.

Not a great number of reviews would or should start off with a comparison to an original Broadway production. Often it would be redundant; by the time a play makes it to the strawhat circuit, the audience is somewhat familiar with the original, especially in the case of hit musicals. Comparing and contrasting the replica with the Broadway original might also appear snobbish or elitist if pushed too far. It is surprising to see how many details are copied faithfully by secondary producers and directors, but it really doesn't have much bearing on the quality of the production.

Here, however, Albrecht has good reason to evoke memories of the original show. The Bucks County Playhouse, near Philadelphia, was among the first professional companies to do *Child's Play* in the year following its successful run on Broadway. When the play opened eighteen months earlier, the *Times* called it "one of the most satisfyingly scary shows in years" and said "the play is immersed in a strange, at first puzzling, atmosphere." All the reviews credited the set, the writing and the acting ensemble for making the melodrama work. And most of the reviews suggested in one way or another that if any of these elements had been less than perfect the play might well have degenerated into something much less. The only sour note in any of the opening night reviews concerned the play's ending, which all the reviewers were willing to overlook in the face of the other considerable attributes.

So Albrecht does not conceive of his task as merely one of judging a production per se. He has the opportunity (and here we have an argument for the important role of criticism far from the Great White Way) to judge a play for the first time on the merits of its suitability for production by typical theater companies throughout the land. *Child's Play* turns out to be too fragile to be performed merely adequately, even by a thoroughly professional group such as that found at Bucks County Playhouse.

After seeing this production, Albrecht felt obliged to take points away from the playwright, who had received the traditional cries of "Author! Author!" on opening night in New York. It often takes a second production to show up the weaknesses of the original which earlier were camouflaged by excellence in set design or a related department.

In the second section of the review, Albrecht explains which directorial decisions harm the play, in his opinion, and which acting nuances work against the desired mood. This raises an obvious question: Do actors and directors adjust anything after reading the first night notices?

If they do, they probably wouldn't admit it. There's just too much pride and vanity involved. An actor might conceivably project better or tone down a harshness that rankled the critics. But there are reasons why many adjustments cannot be made. Installing new lighting cues, altering the blocking of a play, or changing the intonation of lines after a production has been thoroughly rehearsed and "set" (locked in) could be disruptive, even destructive. A play eventually runs machinelike. And as with many machines, tinkering here throws something out of adjustment there. A whole chain reaction can be set off. Most directors choose to ride with minor flaws that have become set rather than risk upsetting the delicate equilibrium of it all.

When there is more than one critic, there will be divergent opinions. So the director or actor who is criticized in one review will find comfort in another. He will listen better, of course, to the critic who tells him everything is going smoothly. (Many actors and directors claim they don't even read the reviews. It just isn't true. Most say they would never change anything they do just because a critic pointed it out. That isn't entirely true, either.)

The critic's suggestions are really more valuable to the actor or director for subsequent productions. After the final curtain is rung down on a show, and as the troupe goes into rehearsal for the next production, some of the suggestions made by the critics may slowly sink in. The director perhaps gains a better notion of what makes farce work; the actor learns that he is more effective when he keeps a rein on excessive mugging, or puts his voice in proper register. The critic rarely is rewarded with an instantaneous change as a result of his suggestions, but he may feel that he has had some small part in helping an actor improve over the years.

The critic of live musical performers has more opportunity, of course, to offer suggestions which may be acted upon directly. The night club, cabaret or exposition hall performer needs suggestions regarding his selection of material, style of presentation, technical aids, and even such things as length of act, costumes and between-music patter.

Albrecht's critique of *Child's Play* followed by one month a similar analysis of the Bucks County production of *Plaza Suite*. In that instance, Albrecht found the show seriously flawed because the actors were playing the roles for the guffaws to be found in Neil Simon's witty one-liners and ignoring almost entirely the characterizations of the protagonists. The critic pointed out that America's favorite comic playwright was striving in his more recent shows to draw three-dimensional characters who are recognizable to the audience and whose problems, fears and worries concern the playgoer.

In his Sunday column the following week, Albrecht pursued the issue further. He expressed concern that, because of Simon's reputation, the plays he wrote would forever be played for easy laughs, ignoring the writer's higher purpose. It is understandable that the critic wrote a disapproving review even though the playhouse had rocked with laughter at the performance he saw: he was genuinely concerned for the development of the playwright and the audience alike.

THE AGONY AND THE ECSTASY

The preceding reviews are typical of the better notices being written currently for the average mass media audience. The writer personally may have liked the plays in question even less than he indicated to the reader, but he has pitched the language and the criticism at a reasonable, instructive level. Although he occasionally voices an opinion in the first person, his criticisms appear to be well meaning and impersonal.

Our examination of styles and approaches would be incomplete, however, if we failed to consider one of the schools of critics found in specialized media—those very personal, no-holds-barred writers who more often than not make a play sound like either an instant Pulitzer Prize winner or the most offensive chunk of grit ever to lodge in the eye of the beholder. Such a critic is John Simon, regularly appearing in the with-it set's *New York* magazine, and also doing battle from time to *Times* in other highbrow media.

Said Simon of *The Trial of the Catonsville Nine:* "I scarcely know how to write about the playwright and his eight co-defendants—how to criticize them. I would simply like to canonize them." After discussing the "grandeur" of the production, he concluded: "If I had a fraction of these people's heroism, I would, at the very least, post myself outside the *No, No, Nanette* box office and beseech prospective customers to buy tickets to this show instead."

His reference to the frothy revival of the 1925 musical called to mind his column of the previous week, where he said in part:

> . . . when I see something like *No, No, Nanette*, I feel like reaching for the nearest plywood gun and rushing to the first street corner to enlist in the guerrilla theater. For though it seems smug and fatuous to make a fetish of mere relevance, reveling in this kind of mindless, soulless and gutless irrelevance is even more offensive . . .
>
> Any way you twist it, *Nanette* is a no-no. And with the mint sunk into producing and promoting this abortion, three young playwrights could have enjoyed useful showcases. The waste! The shame!

Simon isn't content to criticize plays and films; he also criticizes the critics. He attacked the *auteur* theory of *The Village Voice*'s Andrew Sarris in such uncompromising language that the editors of *The New York Times* gave Sarris the opportunity to respond directly in an adjoining piece. The fight rambled on for thousands of words, and in the following weeks the letters column of the *Times* was overflowing with responses. Many of the writers scorned Simon for his personal and vitriolic attack, but some lauded it as a much-needed stripping away of self-granted critical immunity, or at least an opening of a fascinating dialog between critics with opposite viewpoints.

Not many months later, in his *New York* magazine column, Simon prefaced the new Broadway season with an attack on his fellow drama critics, expecially the two men of the *Times*. He accused them, and their paper, of hedging their bets, playing the prejudices of the Old Boy (Kerr) against the prejudices of the New Chap (Barnes) so that there would be an opinion to suit everybody. He knocked all of the New York critics for their "earnest desire to keep show-biz alive, in some form or other, lest they lose their livelihoods." Simon volunteered, unasked, to police his "fellow watchdogs" by criticizing the critics whenever it was called for.

Simon has stated that it is unimportant whether or not the readers agree with the critics. He defines good criticism as writing that makes the audience think, feel and respond. "If we then agree or disagree is less important than the fact that our faculties have been engaged and stretched," Simon believes.

New York magazine enjoys something of a muckraking image and the editors encourage writers in all departments to let the chips fall where they may. But Simon's attacks might not be permitted by the editors of many newspapers, since picking fights is not a usual characteristic of contemporary American journalism. Simon is a loner not so much because he comes by it naturally but more likely because other critics don't feel they have a platform for personal attacks on their colleagues.

That situation would change if Emory Lewis had his way. In *Stages* he laments the blandness of American criticism:

In Europe critics are likely to become involved in colorful quarrels about plays and players. Often critics write with passion from an openly acknowledged stance, and the reader is given, for example, a Catholic, a Communist, and a Fascist view of a particular drama. This is unfamiliar practice in America. Our critics are neither passionate, nor nettlesome, and they usually write from some rather tenuous vantage point called 'objectivity,' whatever that is.

Perhaps the best argument for increased intramural activity among drama critics is the fact that it can create and prolong interest in plays, giving them a chance to find an audience. The current system says, in effect, that all the critics vote after opening night, and the majority wins. An adversary system would give a new play "notices" over a period of weeks or months as the writers attacked and counterattacked in the press. The audience, perhaps stimulated by the arguments among the critics, would be motivated to see the play themselves in order to judge which writer deserved to win the war of words. Most critics, not to mention theater people, would be happy to put the final decision where it belongs: in the hands of the playgoer.

DISCOVERING THE UNCOMMON

If the drama critic's steady diet of three-act comedies were broken only by an occasional musical or the season's lone classic tragedy, he and his writing style would soon atrophy. Fortunately, the critic is usually exposed to dramas which attempt a fresh format or represent something uncommon in modern theater. Innovations challenge the security of the marginally capable reviewer, but they are the godsends that make the job tolerable for the veteran.

Some examples:

When the Folger Theater Group in Washington, D. C., closed out its season with a modern Soviet play, *The Promise* by Aleksei Arbuzov, *Post* critic Richard L. Coe discussed not only the story and the production but also the long trip made by the play from the U. S. S. R. to the U. S. He had seen a performance in Russian during a visit to the ancient Soviet city of Samarkand, as well as the British production which played in New York. The production by the Folger Group was a still different version, but he found the theme intact. He was thus able to make some interesting and valid points about the play, relating it to works by Tolstoy, Chekov and Dostoevski, and commenting upon its relationship to current Soviet fare.

Los Angeles Times drama critic Dan Sullivan saw more than bouncy tunes and witty social comment in the South Coast Repertory's production of *Mother Earth*, a rock musical about ecology. He likened it to *Pins and Needles*, a 1937 revue with a strong trade-union point of view that pricked the conscience and went beyond mere entertainment with its serious underlying message. Before ticking off the entertainment merits of *Mother Earth*, Sullivan placed it closer to Huxley's *Brave New World* than to Orwell's frightening *1984* in the spectrum of future vision. Only in the second half of his review did he mention some of the specific premises and promises of the show, and by then the reader was taking the subject as seriously as the critic wished him to.

A number of more sensitive critics who had the pleasure of watching actor James Whitmore portray the late Will Rogers in a one-man performance at Washington's historic Ford's Theatre noted the message that Rogers' words still held for a contemporary audience. *Saturday Review*'s Henry Hewes summarized: ". . . the total effect of the performance is to remind us rather dramatically how Rogers, who epitomized grass roots American values, was so strongly critical of a government that had very much the same attitudes and failings as our present establishment." While it can be pushed to extremes, the quest for relevance in works representing another era is always part of the critic's task.

P<small>AYING</small> <small>A</small> <small>SECOND</small> <small>CALL</small>

Once a play has been "set" and the complimentary opening night notices have assured it of a long run, the director departs for greener pastures. The ongoing theatrical enterprise is left in the hands of a stage manager, who must use occasional rehearsals and frequent "notes" stuck on actors' mirrors to keep the play in shape.

A few directors return from time to time, but not many. Those who do may not even find themselves welcome. Most stay away because they probably wouldn't like what they might see. In the long run, far too many plays slip a little and some slip a lot. Those that run for more than a major star's contract period—a year, or perhaps as little as six months—may subsequently become the vehicle for a television star who hasn't earned his theatrical battlestripes, or for a comeback candidate who would be better off in a rest home for antiquated thespians.

Of course the theatergoers are still paying $15 top, thinking they'll enjoy the play that was originally reviewed. When they see tattered sets and a wavy chorus line, they may wonder whether the critics knew what they were talking about.

So one of the services—and defense mechanisms—offered by the conscientious critic is the rereview, or call-back notice. Every show should receive one after a year, and whenever there is a major cast change. In difficult roles that place unusual demands on the lead, an understudy may take the matinee performances—another good reason for doing a second review of a play that has already received favorable notice.

Call-backs usually run far shorter than original reviews, perhaps only half a dozen paragraphs. In addition to noting whether the timing is crisp and the show is otherwise intact, the critic has an opportunity to judge whether the play's message or theme holds up on a second viewing. A topical play may be getting rapidly dated; on the other hand, fresh lines may have been substituted to keep it current. Other shows may have depended so much on shock effect, virgin gag lines or a fragile concept that they just don't have as much appeal the second time around. In such cases, the critic must assay the effect of the work on those viewing it for the first time—a good reason for taking along a guest who hasn't seen the play.

Reviewing *Butterflies Are Free* early in its second year, Clive Barnes referred to his own opening night notice as "an admiring but cold rave . . . its very skills perhaps left me a little chilly, and I found its modesty unappealing. The second time, knowing what to expect, I was able to relax more, and to accept that just because a show builds up on laughter and tears as its stock-in-trade it doesn't have to be a corn merchant." He also approved of the second-year cast changes.

A year later, Barnes made his third call and found that the play had "a settled air to it . . . the staging by Milton Katselas has been maintained fairly well, but I must admit that the play is not as effective as it was when it was first put on. . . . This is far too good a Broadway play to have fallen off in this fashion. But the general level of performance is markedly lower than it was on its first night." Barnes also had criticism for the acting style of the venerable Gloria Swanson, who "seems eluded by the part."

One of the benefits of the rereview to the critic, of course, is that it gives him an opportunity to say things he omitted or overlooked the first time around, not to mention the chance for second-guessing oneself and taking another fling at finding the proper adjectives.

10
Films:
The "Now"
Medium

When Stanley Kauffman concluded his collection of film criticism, *A World on Film*, published in 1966, with an essay on "The Film Generation," the term was new and the concept was unfamiliar to many.

Asserting that film is the art for which there is the greatest spontaneous appetite in America today, Kauffman described the new film audience as "the first generation that has matured in a culture in which film has been of accepted serious relevance."

Films such as *The Graduate, Midnight Cowboy, Easy Rider* and *2001: A Space Odyssey* are to the film generation what Salinger, Hemingway and Fitzgerald were to a previous generation. Discussions in high school and college English classes are more likely to center on the Ken Russell film of *Women in Love* than the D. H. Lawrence book. Personal explorations in Super-8 or 16 mm film have replaced the quest for The Great American Novel.

In this climate, film criticism has become not only respectable and widely read but even perhaps the most interesting and consequential sector of critical writing. While the Old Guard maintained the status quo in so many cultural areas during the past decade, entire ranks of filmmakers and film writers came on the scene. Pauline Kael, Judith

Crist, Rex Reed and others rapidly became, if not household words, at least widely known and read and discussed.

The 1960s began with New Wave films that dashed the conventions of Hollywood studio filmmaking, frequently making the camera and the man who hand-held it the true "stars" of the film. Independent production, increasing frankness, and catering to youthful audiences wrought further indelible changes in the cinema industry. Experimental filmmakers working in San Francisco garages and giant corporations hoping to enthrall World's Fair visitors frequently worked on parallel courses—fragmenting, combining, exploding and freezing images in search of new ways to communicate, to experience or to expand the mind.

THE AUTEUR THEORY

Inevitably, the burgeoning field of film criticism generated a new idea—the auteur theory. And, just as inevitably, that theory has become the focal point of the current argument over what film criticism should be.

Attributed to writers in *Cahiers du Cinéma*, France's leading film-theory magazine, and associated most notably in this country with Andrew Sarris of *The Village Voice*, the auteur theory holds that the director is the "author" of the contemporary film, and that it is he who should be at the center of any discussion of the work.

Proponents of the theory make a strong case for it when discussing films controlled from script through shooting to editing by one man: a Godard, a Fellini, a Bergman. The point is still valid when assaying some of Hollywood's great directors, men like Ford, Huston, deMille, Hitchcock and Penn, who have exerted a strong enough influence to remain in control of their films while working under the studio system.

But opponents of the theory consider filmmaking to be a group effort, influenced by many contributors. The source material—best-selling novel or original screenplay—is one element. The work of the cinematographer is another variable. And the performance of the actors is yet another contribution for which the director cannot be given full credit. Add to that the immensely important role of the film editor and other technicians, and it is difficult to attribute the success or failure of a movie to one man, as you might with a book, a painting, a symphony or a solo stage performance.

If disagreement over the auteur theory had merely split the critics and their readers into two clearly defined opposing camps—the *Cahiers* people on one side and the Hollywood technicians on the other—the differences in opinion would not be as interesting as they are. Fortunately for the reader of film criticism, there is a considerable gray area and plenty of people who switch sides from time to time, thus keeping the discussion lively and changing.

Sarris, for example, occasionally jolts people who have come to associate auteurism with artsy foreign directors or trendy and sometimes pretentious American directors. After most critics had dismissed Elia Kazan's potboiler, *The Arrangement*, as an awful, slick, old-fashioned, middlebrow movie, Sarris turned out a rave review that generated heated discussions in film circles for months afterward.

Admitting that *The Arrangement* was, in part, tortured, turgid and overstated, Sarris quickly added: "Nonetheless *The Arrangement* is so completely Kazan's movie that even its weaknesses seem consistent with a vision of life that is supposed to have died in the '50s." And later: "Kazan reminds us that however blurred his vision, he has been where it's at, and that in his own life he has come back from the brink of oblivion on his own terms and with his own memories." Most of the review dealt with Kazan's life, Kazan's vision, Kazan's thematic and stylistic similarity to Fellini, and (as the child's review of a longish book on penguins is supposed to have concluded) "more than we want to know about" Kazan.

When auteur theorists find so much to praise—indeed, so much to *say*—about a picture that the majority of critics have dismissed as decidedly mediocre, the derogatory label "film buff" is frequently leveled at them. The Buff, of course, is one who loves films, film stars and the film experience so thoroughly that he is out of touch with the interests and standards of the larger audience. Worse, he is immediately defensive, rejecting out of hand any criticism except that with which he agrees.

IF NOT THE AUTEUR, WHAT?

Because the majority of audience members are not interested in the auteur theory, most movie reviewers for the mass media instead approach a film with two general questions in mind: Is it good entertainment? Does it help us understand ourselves or the world around us better?

"Good entertainment" is what the movies always provided in the 1930s and 1940s—love stories, adventure, excitement, exotic locales. By the end of the 1950s, however, such escapist fare was out of vogue in the cinema, partly because the audience was more sophisticated, but mainly because the same stuff was provided free and in great abundance by commercial television. When a "family" picture occasionally surfaced in the 1960s' sea of serious, often pretentious, adult fare, it was usually packaged in wide screen and sold at road show prices in order to lure audiences with the promise of a "special entertainment event" not available on television.

So it has come to the point where critics feel they have to apologize, in effect, for the fact that a movie is "nothing but a happy, tune-filled two hours when you can forget your worries and cares" or "a simple story of young love, not a bad way to pass a summer evening." At $3 a ticket, plus five bucks for the baby-sitter, and perhaps everything else in your pockets for the muggers, maybe "good entertainment" isn't a valid enough reason for venturing out at night.

Thus most critics are looking for the second attribute, relevance or "importance." (Imagine advertising a movie as "important" back in the 1940s—people would have stayed away in droves.) If the theme is drug addiction, homosexual love, alienation from modern society, or a revolutionary change of government, the contemporary critic is in his element. The review arranges itself nicely around an essay on the issue or the problem, and how intelligent viewers might react to it.

Stanley Kauffman, handling two films in a single review, fashioned an essay about the coming of age of movies with racial themes:

In a negative way *A Raisin in the Sun* and *Take a Giant Step* are milestones in the social history of the American Negro. Both films are shoddy, and the happy fact is that today there is no compunction to praise them simply because they are well-intended works by Negroes. Too much has been accomplished in the artistic life of our country by such people as James Baldwin, Ralph Ellison, Richard Wright, Gwendolyn Brooks, and Langston Hughes (to name only a few) to permit patronization of these motion pictures because they happen to be by and about Negroes.

Kauffman then went on to dismiss the films as "commonplace." In a similar vein, Pauline Kael rejected the theme and treatment of *The Chase*:

This is a hate-the-white-South movie. If you turned it around and showed Negroes doing what the White Southerners in the movie do, every Negro organization and civil rights group would have good cause to protest. The newest scapegoats are White Southerners; this time it's the liberals who are doing it, and they're using the oldest device—showing the White Southerners as sexually obsessed.

Reviewing Eric Rohmer's film *Claire's Knee* in the *Los Angeles Times*, Charles Champlin endeavored to apprise readers of the ways in which the French director manages to capture the most subtle shadings of human relationships:

> Nothing much happens. A girl is kissed and both partners see that the game has gone far enough. A girl is told a cruel truth, but the teller is more cruelly hurt than the told. But what does happen feels disturbingly loud in the summer stillness, and in the reserved exchanges one senses that the characters have been revealed to themselves and to each other with sharp and uncomfortable clarity . . . morality is of course the sum of the guidelines for our relations with others, and, like liberty, it is indivisible. What Rohmer is suggesting is that cruelties come in all sizes.

Reviewing a Rohmer film—even if one focuses on the theme and the technique—necessarily leads to at least a blending of auteur and traditional criticism. His six "moral tales" are thematically interrelated films, and it is impossible to avoid discussing the director's filmography. Champlin provided the obligatory background, and he compared *Claire's Knee* with the recently distributed *My Night at Maud's*. But otherwise he strived to evaluate the film on its own merits.

ANALYZING THE FILM REVIEW

The following review by Jay Cocks appeared in *Time* magazine:

> Alex is a young and abruptly successful film director whose somewhat desultory wanderings through his subconscious and Hollywood form the core of *Alex in Wonderland*, a movie that appears to be a looking-glass portrait of its director, Paul Mazursky. Like his protagonist, Mazursky achieved rapid success recently with *Bob and Carol and Ted and Alice* and, like Alex again, he was alternately baffled, delighted and finally stymied by his success. Unlike Alex, however, Mazursky found a way out of his creative quandary: he and coauthor Larry Tucker simply fictionalized and embellished it slightly, then filmed it. The result, although unsuccessful overall, is frequently funny, nasty and telling—better by several light-years than *Bob and Carol* and a lot more honest in the bargain.
>
> The model for such a cinematic self-portrait, of course, is Federico

Fellini's masterpiece *8½*, and *Alex* includes an almost obsessional number of homages to the maestro. The best is a meeting between Alex and Fellini, who is working on his new TV film *The Clowns*, and who politely but firmly excuses himself from Alex's overawed gushings. Fellini, to absolutely no one's surprise, turns out to be quite an actor, and the scene is a gem. But Alex-Mazursky is no Fellini, and *Alex* is not *8½*. Fellini's film was the testament of a frustrated genius; *Alex* is merely the sketch of a temporarily thwarted artisan.

Mazursky's fantasy sequences—save for a comic nightmare about war on Hollywood Boulevard—are decidedly earthbound. More seriously, his attitude toward Hollywood alternates between ridicule and a weird kind of arm's-length respect. He neatly and hilariously skewers one of those groovy new Hollywood studio executives (played and flayed to a turn by Mazursky himself) but his attitude toward Hollywood's pseudo-intellectuals and revolutionary Malibu poseurs is benignly sun-kissed. The film's ending, which features Alex talking over his problems with a tree in back of his newly bought house, is not so much ambiguous as confused.

Donald Sutherland's performance as the bedeviled Alex is his most complex and fully developed to date. He is so shrewdly, quietly excellent that he gives Alex more depth—and certainly a good deal more sympathy—than he might otherwise have had. Ellen Burstyn, as Alex's dedicated but sometimes edgy wife, is lovely and affecting; and there are a lot of good cameo appearances by everyone from Jeanne Moreau to Mazursky's two daughters.

Alex is not the best of the Hollywood-on-Hollywood movies. (Preston Sturges' *Sullivan's Travels*, made back in 1941, is still the one to beat.) Mazursky can be faulted for pretension and presumption in assuming that an audience would be interested in his creative and familial trials. But he is also a man of talent, shrewd perceptions and a good deal of grating honesty—enough to make *Alex* an ego trip that is often fun along the way. ("Portrait of an Artisan" reprinted by permission from *Time*, the weekly newsmagazine; © Time, Inc., 1971).

Many readers may find this review irritating. The piece is a mosaic of elements. A rereading is necessary in order to discern the structure; even the casual reader might find himself rereading certain sentences and paragraphs in order to decide whether the comments were favorable or unfavorable. This is not to fault the reviewer. The film, like so many produced at the beginning of the 1970s, is loosely structured and often elusive—like the little girl with the little curl, very good when it is good, and not so good when it is bad. To cut through it all with a tidy essay might impose an orderliness or neatness that would do the film an injustice.

On rereading, and after seeing the film, it is obvious that Cocks really did manage, in just five paragraphs, to put his finger on the film's strengths and weaknesses, at the same time giving the "feel" of the film and putting it in some sort of context.

The heart of the matter is found squarely at the midpoint of the review: *Alex in Wonderland,* while striving to emulate the testament of a frustrated genius, is merely the sketch of a temporarily thwarted artisan. The skim reader looking for the yea-or-nay verdict has it clearly enough here. But because the film is busy going off in so many directions, the review must inevitably counterbalance a great number of pros and cons:

PRO: The film is "several light-years" better than *Bob and Carol and Ted and Alice,* which was a popular movie. A scene with Fellini is "a gem." The director does a neat turn himself, "hilariously" skewering studio executives. The acting is uniformly good. The film is "often fun along the way"—the final phrase, which is where many readers expect the box score, is complimentary.

CON: The film is a portrait of its director (yawn) and is "unsuccessful overall." The fantasy sequences are prosaic. The director's attitude wavers. The ending is "confused." The film doesn't stand up to the best of the genre. The director is guilty of some pretension and presumptuousness.

In addition to ticking off these counterbalancing characteristics, the reviewer provides—inadvertently, because of the mirror qualities of the film—a discussion of the director's role that should satisfy the auteurist. Thus the review, in its relatively short space, manages to be many things to many people.

PITCHING IT TO THE READER

Because theater is for theatergoers, classical music is for music lovers, and so on, criticism in those fields pitches itself to the same audience, regardless of the communications medium, in which it appears. That is, it is aimed at the typical consumer of the entertainment form rather than at the typical consumer of the communications vehicle.

The movies, however, are an extremely democratic and eclectic entertainment/art form. There are pornographic movies, children's movies, women's movies, men's movies and, more important, movies that aim for lowbrow, middlebrow or highbrow audiences. The demographics of moviegoing are similar enough to the demographics of newspaper reading that many reviewers in the daily press can feel with conviction, "This is the kind of movie my readers like" or, conversely, "This may go over big with a certain audience, but it surely isn't going to interest the type of people who read our paper."

The premise was well supported when two films concerning cross-country automobile chases opened simultaneously in New York. The reactions of the reviewers on the city's two leading papers reflected their concepts of the readership.

The plebeian *Daily News* called *Two-Lane Blacktop* "a drag all the way," curtly disposing of it in 170 words. The reviewer was befuddled by the tale. She admitted to her Rheingold-swigging Middle American readers that she couldn't figure out why, during the peculiar race between three young people and an older man, the contestants purposely slowed up and even helped repair one another's automobiles.

Over at the patrician *Times*, however, critic Vincent Canby was hardly befuddled: after all, he had already read the screenplay in *Esquire* and recognized the metaphorical aspirations of the filmmakers. He found it "a remarkably engaging movie" and concluded that it was made "with the restraint and control of an aware, mature filmmaker."

The day's second film, *The Last Run*, had George C. Scott and another bad guy fleeing across Spain, pursued by even badder guys. Roger Greenspun of the *Times* found the handling of the material so disagreeable ("a decent enough project that has been rendered ludicrous . . . more by directorial misjudgement than by any necessity in the screenplay") that he could find no redeeming worth in the acting. Acknowledging his admiration for Oscar-winner Scott, the reviewer averred that the actor had merely opted to do the director's bidding instead of interpreting the role.

The *News* critic didn't particularly like the story, either, but there any similarity to the *Times* review ended. The piece dealt with Scott's acting job:

> He is, at all times, the complete master of his material; adding much-needed punch to the lines with his cynical, dry delivery and thus building up his tough-guy role into a sympathetic portrait of a dried up, beaten man who wants just one more chance to prove he's alive.

107

That description is bound to ring some sort of bell with the typical working-class reader of the *News* whose dreams and fantasies, when they are not centered on the Daily Double at Belmont or the Instant Millionaire drawing in the state lottery, have to do with "just one more chance" to gather the old bones together and be something in life.

The *News* review makes no mention of the director upon which the *Times* put most of the blame. A look at the entertainment pages of the *News* shows why. The paper is overflowing with old-fashioned gossip columns jammed with item after item about What the Hollywood Stars are Saying and Doing. No wonder the entire review tells of Scott's role, Scott's performance. The critic, to her credit, knows what will interest and involve her two million readers.

Alien to the typical subscribers of both the *Times* and the *News* would be some of the more far-out reviews carried in *The Village Voice*. Consider the central paragraph in David Ehrenstein's ode to the Godard film about (about?) the Rolling Stones, *Sympathy for the Devil*, also distributed as *One Plus One* with a different ending (ending?):

How can I explain how the back of Brian Jones' head looks? Or what that look means? Or the effect achieved when the narrator at that point suddenly announces 'Page 75'? Perhaps I can say that the image is icy cool, but that would explain little. It would not explain the meaning of the exciting moment when Godard pans away to two gorgeous lights (red and blue) near the recording room's ceiling. It would not explain that the space the camera traverses in the recording studio is more important than what is in the studio itself (i.e., the Stones). It would not explain why a tracking shot is a moral statement. (Outside of the brief shots of Anne Wiazemsky, all the sequences are tracking shots.) It would not explain. Explain?

No need to explain. Readers of the *Voice* understand why it is essential that the back of Brian Jones' head remains forever a mystery.

VÉRITÉ . . . AND OTHER REALITIES

One of the most exciting, vital and increasingly popular branches of commercial moviemaking is—to borrow a term from book publishing—the "nonfiction" film. In the past, they were usually called "documentaries," a label which too often became synonymous with "boring" as a result of the relentlessly instructive nature of the films. In recent years, *cinéma vérité* has been the category most in vogue, suggesting that a truth or reality resulted from spontaneity on the part of the filmmaker.

Al Maysles (*Salesman* and *Gimme Shelter*) prefers the term "direct cinema" to describe films which deal with actual events in real time (as opposed to time condensed or expanded), without interposing either a script or a director's predetermined interpretation. Allan King (*Warrendale* and *A Married Couple*) calls it "actuality" drama.

The critic who divides all films into either fiction or nonfiction and then thinks of all nonfiction films as documentaries is going to be in trouble when he tries to analyze the purpose of a movie, the director's role and the ultimate effectiveness of the work. In the past decade, at least half a dozen subgenres have emerged:

(1) The direct cinema/actuality drama of the Maysles brothers, King and only a few others. This is "mouse-in-the-corner" moviemaking, although the mouse must bring lights, sound equipment and at least two or three 16mm cameras. Real people permit their comings and goings to be filmed, and the hope is that some higher truth will emerge. The subjects of the film are usually ordinary people with whom the viewers can identify—a hustling Middle American Bible salesman trying to achieve success through drive and determination, or a couple whose marriage is breaking up. The structure of the film is frequently "a typical day/week in the life of" the subjects. The producer-director's creative role is theoretically limited to (a) selecting a subject and a situation that promise to generate something valid and interesting, and (b) editing anywhere from 30 to 100 hours of footage down to a two-hour film that is representative of the totality.

(2) The assemblage of assorted related footage into a coherent study of some sociological phenomenon. At its worst, this category yields a *Mondo Cane* or one of that film's obscene offshoots. More representative is *Groupies*, which assembled vignettes of the fans who follow the rock bands on tour in hopes of going to bed with them. The "assemblage" film may have a narrator, or it may rely on visual transitions to tie the sequences together.

(3) The "total assault" documentary. The National Football League was quick to learn that dramatic, exciting events can be further exploited if a large team of professionals is assembled to capture footage for a slick, polished recreation. The NFL Films technicians

use upbeat music, terse narration and flashy editing techniques to great advantage. A championship game, a team's entire season, or highlights of one facet of the sport are condensed into a half-hour film with considerable impact and appeal. Rock concert promoters used the same techniques to turn losses at the gate into profits at the movie-theater box offices. *Woodstock, The Film* revealed that not everybody was lounging in the mud at that incredible festival. Teams of photographers and sound men were recording it for later editing into a split-screen extravaganza that *was* the event for millions of young people. (Note the full title of the movie: *The Film* implies that the cinematic event is distinct and separate from the event it chronicles.)

(4) The semidocumentary, or documentarylike exposition of a lifestyle. Bruce Brown's *Endless Summer* used the "search for the perfect wave" as a loose dramatic peg for his stunning moving pictures of surfing around the world. There was no message, no great or important truth to be discovered by the audience, as with Maysles or King. Later, Brown did much the same thing for motorcycle racing in *On Any Sunday*. Robert Kaylor's *Derby* structured its narrative around the escapades of one real-life flamboyant roller derby star, but actually the *context* was the focal point of the film, not the protagonist. *Blue Water, White Death* chronicled the underwater photographer's pursuit of the great white shark; the film was, in effect, a successful extension of the home movie that asks the audience to "look at the excitement we had."

(5) The political documentary. This form, until recently unfamiliar to American audiences, often combines newsreel footage with film clips from speeches or rallies, and perhaps even restaged interpretations of incidents vital to a political line. Such films may espouse a cause and propagandize favorably for a leader (*Fidel*) or they may take a point of view on a controversial issue (*The Murder of Fred Hampton*).

(6) The fiction film which uses the techniques of the documentary or *cinéma vérité*. Just as the nonfiction film frequently affects a story line in order to achieve organizational unity, a fiction film may imitate the documentary in order to provide a feeling of realism. *Taking Off*, which dealt with youthful runaways, took off with an extended sequence at an audition that presented young singers without makeup, without coaching and, in some cases, without inhibition. The lead

roles in the film were taken by improvisational actors who, while working from a script, gave the appearance of experiencing the hurts and surprises as they went along. *The Andromeda Strain* achieved its quasi-documentary feeling by focusing more on the technology of the top secret Project Wildfire than on any one of the humans involved in the chilling science-fiction story.

Critics who feel secure enough about their grasp of literature and their comprehension of filmmaking techniques may feel slightly less secure when the occasional nonfiction film comes along. Al Maysles has stated that most critics are oriented to the fiction film and have no understanding of how and why nonfiction films are made. "They assume we want to be fiction filmmakers, which is wrong," he lamented after several film writers questioned the methods used in *Gimme Shelter*.

Here, perhaps, is the best example of a situation in which the critic is right to conceive of himself as "a typical member of the audience." The nonfiction film is made as an *informational* film before all else, whether that information is light or heavy, objectively or subjectively presented. The critic, therefore, can profitably abandon his authoritative stance and take a more impressionistic viewpoint. He may raise the question: What does this tell us about ourselves or our society that helps us to understand ourselves better? And he may react in a purely contemporaneous way: Why does this interest us, and how does it inform us at this moment in our development?

One of the issues frequently raised about the nonfiction film is the invasion of the privacy of those who are filmed. Andrew Sarris was particularly critical of the exploitation of *Groupies:*

There is an implied moral commitment in filmmaking even to people suffering from self-hatred. We are not morally entitled to shoot a person who says he wants to die, and neither is a director morally entitled to degrade a person who wishes to make a fool of himself.

Another question often raised is the authenticity of supposedly candid, unrehearsed subjects. Vincent Canby discussed the problem in his review of *A Married Couple:*

. . . it's perfectly apparent that Billy and Antoinette are playing to the camera, in moments of anger, intimacy and even boredom. It may be no accident that both of them were, at earlier stages in their lives, aspiring actors who never made it. The unreality prompted by the camera's presence is acknowledged in the film, which then proceeds to pass off this conscious performance as some kind of metatruth that is neither fact nor fiction.

Time magazine's reviewer felt obliged to note that the director's own marriage was breaking up during the editing of *A Married Couple* and speculated that it may have influenced his selection and arrangement of events. It can be seen that the nonfiction film, in its quest for "simple truth," can provide a complex task for the reviewer who wants to go beyond its surface realities.

THE LIFE AND TIMES OF . . .

Two issues are paramount in judging the film biography. Is the characterization of the individual accurate and honest? Is there something to be gained by exhuming the life and times of the central figure?

Film biographies are popular because they deal with persons we know about and are interested in, and also because they provide worthy starring vehicles for our leading actors. Of course, Tayloring a role to fit the star (or Burtoning it) can lead to distortion, so it is incumbent upon the critic to prepare adequately for reviewing films based on historical fact.

The most successful and acclaimed "biog" of recent years was *Patton* (full title, significantly, *Patton: Salute to a Rebel*). The critics agreed almost to the man that George C. Scott's acting triumph did not come at the expense of the World War Two general's reputation. A major exception was *Time* magazine, which opined that "the movie's vision blurs the man" in its drive to prove him the rebel of the title.

The vast majority of writers found the characterization faithful and the film's underlying message relevant to a 1970 America torn between antimilitarism and superpatriotism. "The overall impact of the film is its penetrating and perceptive study of a man whose character is amazingly pertinent to our understanding of the past and present," wrote Judith Crist. Hollis Alpert in *Saturday Review* cited the film as a study of "command mentality" vital to contemporary audiences because "it is of importance for us to know what makes men like Patton tick."

Several major reviewers, perhaps surprised by a certain self-betrayal of attitudes on their own part (which is how the film affected many antiwar liberals), attempted to get a fix on the under-lying inclinations of the producers. At a number of points in his original review, Vincent Canby dealt with the issue. First he labeled the film an "initially ambivalent but finally adoring . . . portrait." Later he concluded that the producers and script writers "have quite mixed feelings about Patton, but they are ultimately denied by the epic (reverential) treatment." Canby came back to the issue once more in his Sunday column, stating that the opinion to be garnered about Patton depended ultimately on the audience member's individual point of view. What was more important, in the long run, was that the film portrait was "consistently fascinating," Canby wrote.

Fascination—with royalty, with power, and worst of all with costumes and pageantry—is often what ruins film biography, reducing it to mere spectacle. *Cromwell,* with its unrestrained overacting and carefully detailed battle extravaganzas, was cited by one reviewer as the triumph of the technical adviser, not the filmmaker. Likewise, *Anne of the Thousand Days* (which won awards from the Hollywood technicians, if not from the critics) was more a collection of English royalty clichés and pseudoprofundities about kingly powers than a study of motivation or a dramatization of human relationships.

Inevitably, some film biographers have come to believe that the most sophisticated moviegoers of today are willing and able to go beyond historical accuracy into the realm of psychoanalytical characterizations, or even surrealistic fantasy. Ken Russell's *The Music Lovers* appears to make the point that a tormenting sex life (or the lack of one) was directly responsible for the vigorous music of Tchaikovsky. After watching cannons shoot off the heads of the composer's immediate circle of tormentors to the rollicking chords of the *1812 Overture,* some critics could only call it a desecration. A few, however, were willing to concede Russell a spirited interpretation, rewarding enough to compensate for such indulgences.

ACKNOWLEDGING THE SOURCE

One of the most frequent obligations of the film critic is the acknowledgment of source material. Even in this era of personal, independent filmmaking and directorial domination, the majority of films are adapted from other forms—usually novels and plays, but also short stories, nonfiction writing and television.

An excellent appraisal of a story's transfer from one medium to another was provided by Renata Adler in her Sunday *Times* essay on *The Graduate:*

The script is quite faithful to the novel of the same title by Charles Webb. The difference is that the book is written quite clearly from the viewpoint of the Graduate, his perspective, his distortions, his caricatures of his elders and of himself. One can adjust to that perspective, make allowances for it, figure out more or less automatically what the reality was. . . . Movies are a more autocratic form; and when *The Graduate*, after beginning as a straight, beautifully made Mike Nichols satire, takes on almost imperceptibly the viewpoint of its major character—becomes afraid with him, for example, of Anne Bancroft and begins to see her as a villainess in a melodrama—it is, in conventional movie terms, very puzzling. Particularly since the acting is so good. Everyone becomes as the Graduate sees him, and only people who share his view of the world can really be completely satisfied with the film after that.

When films adapted from other sources fail, it is often because the story material is still partly bound to the conventions of the original medium. Film is visual; film is more condensed than a book, more fluid than a play; the film experience is not quite like any other even when the subject matter is identical. "They followed the story in the book" may be a condemnation rather than a compliment. A number of critics noted the differences between the stage and screen versions of *Entertaining Mr. Sloane*. A graveyard scene and several death rituals involving a corpse were added in the movie. They might have seemed ludicrous on stage, where the crisp dialog and interplay between the characters was the stuff of the evening. But they worked marvelously when distorted by the lens, magnified out of proportion by camera angle, and enhanced by editing. The effects of the play and of the film were somewhat different, but each was appropriate to its medium.

II
TV:
What's on the
Tube Tonight?

America's foremost critic of television doesn't work for a newspaper or a magazine, although his articles appear frequently in the leading periodicals. Outspoken Federal Communications Commissioner Nicholas Johnson has "single-handedly undertaken to reform U. S. television," in the words of columnist William F. Buckley, Jr.

In his book *How to Talk Back to Your Television Set*, Johnson estimates that the viewer spends the equivalent of nine full years of his life in front of the tube. In the typical home, the television set is watched almost six hours each day, he notes. And what does Johnson think of the way television fills those thousands of viewing hours?

Given the great unfulfilled needs that television could serve in this country and is not serving, given the great evil that the evidence tends to suggest it is presently doing, one can share the judgment of the late Senator Robert Kennedy that television's performance is, in a word, "unacceptable."

Would that words so strong had flowed from the typewriters of the print media's television critics for the past two decades; perhaps then the tube would not be the "vast wasteland" deplored by Newton Minow at the beginning of the 1960s.

Much of what was written about television in the daily newspapers and the mass circulation magazines during the medium's formative years, however, was uncritical flackery akin to the loving attention lavished on sports, movies and fads in dress. Instead of reviewers, the public was given "TV columnists," many of whom willingly took all-expense-paid champagne junkets to the television serial mills in and around Los Angeles. During the season premieres of the new sitcoms and Western adventure shows, how could they help but wax enthusiastic? After all, they had met the stars during the filming or taping of the first thirteen installments; they were virtually insiders, part of the project. The idiot viewers were apparently supposed to get some sort of vicarious thrill out of the flack columnist's experiences.

It was 1967 before the nation's leading news magazine created an exclusive section to examine all aspects of what the editors belatedly recognized as television's "pervasive influence." Even today, most newspapers use bland, all-purpose syndicated and wire service material to fill the space around the program listings. The Associated Press critic dial-twists throughout the evening, attempting to "cover" television fare much as a reporter would cover a city council meeting. A "special" or documentary gets lead play—perhaps six or eight paragraphs. Other programs of interest (frequently installments of musical variety shows; sometimes even episodes of half-hour comedy shows) receive briefer notice. Often these mentions, as edited by the local papers, amount to little more than the retelling of a joke or a nice comment on the performance by a guest star.

Perhaps network television, being something of an opiate for the masses, deserves the cursory glance it gets from the print media. Critic Jack Gould of *The New York Times* has questioned his own role and that of the tube's other intellectual and highly educated viewers: "Who can be so bold as to suggest that his own values are the only valid ones and that people in different circumstances don't see TV in different terms?" He cited a college president who relaxed watching sports events, a laborer who unwound in front of escapist fare, and a black mother in the South who praised television because the announcers speak better English than her children hear in school.

Certainly the critic's task is not to turn the tube into a Metropolitan Opera House or a Carnegie Hall. But as *Variety*, the voice of show business, pointed out at the beginning of the 1970–71 season, the old "habit audience" is waning. Viewers are growing increasingly unwilling to sit through the predictable situations and stock characters week after week. In coming years television will be a medium in transition, offering new forms of programming. In this context, the role of the reviewer will doubtless be much more important than it has been in the past.

The TV critic's "stance"

The critic in each medium, as mentioned in an earlier chapter, must define his "stance"—his position regarding the audience, the performer, the producer. His accessibility to the art form, his audience's particular needs, and the demands of the medium in which his work appears all combine to dictate that stance.

The *Washington Star*'s Bernie Harrison once characterized television critics as "spokesmen for the viewers" who act as gadflies, forcing everybody involved in the communications field—including Congress and the FCC—to work for improvements. *Los Angeles Times* writer Hal Humphrey credits his fellow television columnists with cajoling the networks into preempting daytime quiz shows and soap operas for important debates and votes at the United Nations.

In his excellent book of critical essays on television, *The Living Room War*, Michael Arlen assails early reviewers of the medium for focusing their attention on programming. Arlen, whose blunt opinions appear in *The New Yorker*, was one of the first television critics to concentrate on the *effects* of television instead of merely the *content*. Since television is a reflection of society, he postulated, "television criticism must be a criticism of the whole society." The best reviewers today are those who understand this concept and approach their task accordingly.

Assessing documentaries about the nation's drug addiction problem, for example, the best reviewers went beyond the scope of the program under consideration and asked some penetrating questions of the networks: Why do you air this program at 10 p.m. in a documentary format? The problem is most acute among younger viewers; it is imperative that they be reached in a different format at a different time. Why do you focus on the exotic drugs such as marijuana and heroin, ignoring completely the fact that many of your own programs carry advertisements for habit-forming "legal" sedatives, tranquilizers, pep pills and the like? Why do you base your information entirely on interviews with medical and legal authorities who offer only medical explanations and legal solutions to what is also a social and moral problem? The issues raised by these questions reflect the competent reviewer's comprehension of the big picture, not just of what appears on the small screen.

In the opening chapter we looked at the many ways in which the critic serves his public. The special duties of the television reviewer should be added here.

(1) He reinforces experience.

The drama critic attends an opening night performance along with a few hundred other persons. If he gives favorable notice, the public will continue to patronize the offering in successive groups of several hundred. But the television reviewer watches a program along with millions of his countrymen, and what he has to say about it is very much after the fact. He speaks to the "consumer" after the purchase is made, not before.

That doesn't mean that his work is redundant. Instead, it has a primary purpose not found in most kinds of reviewing—that of reinforcing experience. Viewers enjoy matching their own reactions against those of a qualified judge. If opinions agree, they are pleased. If opinions disagree, they might well learn to be more discerning. At the very least, they will have had their sensibilities nudged—even if their reaction is to sit down and fire off a lambasting letter to the editor.

Perhaps the most useful reinforcement is the augmentation of educational and informative programs. After absorbing a plethora of facts and ideas, the viewer comes to appreciate the short half-life of knowledge. It is helpful to find the most telling items recounted in the following day's review, along with summary and evaluation.

Here, for example, is a segment of Jack Gould's report in *The New York Times* on CBS's controversial Emmy Award-winning documentary, *The Selling of the Pentagon:*

[The program] . . . was not long in getting to the point: The Pentagon now admits to spending $30-million a year on 'public affairs' on the home front. Mr. Mudd said that an unpublished report by the 20th Century Fund suggests that the true total may turn out to be $190-million.
The program cited the annual ritual of Armed Forces Day, when

civilians are seated in grandstands to see combat units put on a show. The complaints of mothers about their children buying toy guns paled into comparative irrelevancy. Thanks to the Pentagon, youngsters could play with real guns and sit in real tanks.

Too often, newspaper editors fail to realize that what happens on television may be legitimate news, worthy of front page coverage. An excellent documentary may be as newsworthy as a presidential press conference or a championship sports event. It is the reviewer's duty to recognize the news value and call it to the attention of his editors. Television reporting should not be relegated automatically to the entertainment pages.

(2) He alerts the viewer to watch for worthwhile reruns.

It is a monument to network selfishness and greed that very few programs are previewed for the critics. Closed-circuit screenings are a simple matter to arrange. CBS has periodically invoked such a policy, but it is fair to say that commercial television prefers to corral the largest possible audience with incessant promotion in order to deliver X million viewers to the sponsor at the appointed time. That attitude precludes prior criticism. Fortunately, television writers like *The New York Times*'s John J. O'Connor are beginning to assail the practice:

> Unfortunately for viewers who don't pay much attention to the program listings, one of the more valuable, and valuably disturbing, of recent news specials slipped almost unheralded last night onto the home screens served by the National Broadcasting Company. 'This Child Is Rated X—An N.B.C. News White Paper on Juvenile Justice' was precisely the type of television program that merits advance discussion and recommendation. But for various ornate reasons N.B.C. has a policy against the pre-reviewing of its programs. Go fight N.B.C.

Most hour-long specials are costly and not immediately perishable, so they invariably reappear as spring and summer reruns. The reviewer should indicate to those who missed the program whether or not it is worth watching for later. Another fault of the majority of newspaper television pages is that little attempt is made to call attention to repeat showing of important programs. Once again, the reviewer must take the initiative, finding space in his column to reiterate his reactions to the initial airing. Eventually cassette television will make it possible for the viewer to borrow tapes of programs from the public library or a rental service, at which time the reviewer's role will become much more analogous to that of the book critic.

(3) He rewards excellence.

The one-shot nature of television programming and the reluctance of networks to permit previews do restrict the reviewer's influence. Yet he has some not inconsiderable power: he can encourage or discourage the producers—and indirectly the sponsors—with his reward of praise or his penalty of disapprobation. A popular anecdote holds that CBS Chairman of the Board William Paley once cancelled a European vacation in reaction to an influential columnist's attack on the insipidness of the network's programming. And even sponsors who seek the most mediocre audience cannot ignore an attack that mentions their name along with that of the offending producer. The American penchant for "good public relations" inevitably penetrates the most calloused commercial hide.

The reviewer of popular television fare should not underestimate the importance of his evaluative input. If rating systems and the personal tastes of the sponsors were the only indexes, television might never lift itself above its comfortable lowbrow level. The reviewer, however, can be the voice of conscience heard in the boardroom over the din of profitability and the clamor for mass appeal.

PREPARATION AND BACKGROUND FOR TV REVIEWING

Television calls for the most eclectic of reviewers. He may be called upon to watch Brecht on Public Broadcasting and then switch to a commercial channel in time to catch a frothy Burt Bacharach special. The very small minority of excellent newspapers assign the regular drama critic to handle the Brecht, leaving Bacharach to the entertainment columnist. Some editors wisely assigned the task of reviewing Paul Newman's *Once Upon a Wheel*, auto-racing special to the sports department. But typically a lone reviewer must equip himself to handle everything that comes along. The simultaneous scheduling of special programs by two networks occasionally makes the reviewer's task virtually impossible (another reason why previews would be useful!).

Most documentaries and special productions are scheduled months in advance. The print media are then deluged with promotional material, mostly light features and publicity stills. In addition, it is desirable for the conscientious reviewer to prepare himself and his readers adequately and independently, instead of leaning entirely on handouts.

When the NET Playhouse "Biography" series presented a program on dancer Isadora Duncan, for example, there was much a critic could do to prepare for the event:

He might, upon discovering that the program was originally created for the British Broadcasting Corporation, seek out reports in the British press.

Observing that the director of the program was Ken Russell, whose films (*Women in Love, The Music Lovers*) generated strong comment, he might profitably assemble information about Russell's approach to classic stories and biographies.

It would be wise for him to set down reactions to the characterization of Isadora Duncan rendered by the estimable British actress Vanessa Redgrave in the film version of the dancer's life.

And, of course, he could repair to the nearest library for additional biographical material.

For the Hallmark Hall of Fame presentation of *Hamlet*, starring Richard Chamberlain, reviewers were provided with a sizable packet of information by the network. Statements by the producer, the director and the star attempted to explain why the play was given a 19th-century setting, how it was cut from four to two hours, and how it was that an American of comparatively limited experience came to find himself in one of the theater's most demanding roles.

In assaying Hallmark's *Hamlet*, the critics had to address themselves to diverse questions. How does this *Hamlet* compare with other *Hamlets?* That is the question one must first answer about every *Hamlet*. But, further, how does the production adapt itself to the special requirements of the medium and to the realities of the television audience's ability to absorb classic drama? When Sir Laurence Olivier's 1948 film version of the play was shown, uninterrupted by commercial messages, from 9 p.m. to midnight by a New York station, the audience was forced to make its own intermissions or sit still for three hours, and the critics protested. Of the Chamberlain version, critic Gould noted:

The Hallmark Company is to be thanked for financing two hours of Shakespeare, but hopefully its advertising agency will become more aware there are ample natural breaks even in a fore-shortened version of 'Hamlet' and that middle commercials have no place in the middle of scenes. Such thoughtfulness would not affect sales response; on the contrary, it would enhance consumer concentration without introducing an element of resentment.

It is useful for the television critic to have some familiarity with the technical limitations and possibilities of the medium. Most colleges offer courses in television production, and there are enough books on the subject. However the reviewer equips himself to understand the medium, what matters is that he must be able to offer valid and constructive criticism of the uses to which it is put. One of the finest analyses of video peculiarities constituted the lead paragraphs of *New York Times* television writer Fred Ferreti's reaction to the debut of *The Great American Dream Machine* on the Public Broadcasting Service network:

Television, real television, came at last to television last night in 'The Great American Dream Machine.' It's been a long time coming.

Too much of television is radio programs with pictures. Too much of what passes for television news is the unimaginative transmission of predictable images. Too much of what is considered TV drama or TV entertainment is scaled-down theater done on television sound stages. In short, most of what Americans see on television is not television, but simply other media dropping by for visits.

The strength of television lies in spontaneity, in instant impressions: in the ability to stun, to shock, to amuse, to annoy, to anger, forcing the viewer from reaction to reaction with infinite ease. The uniqueness of television lies in its ability to fade in and out, to pervade, to influence without seeming to.

Television, real television, is 'San Francisco Mix,' not vaudeville variety. It's 'Sesame Street,' not 'Romper Room.' It's live football with all its attendant violence, not the edited 'Game of the Week.' Television is covering breaking news live with film and tape units; everything else is newsreels. 'The Great American Dream Machine' is television . . . and what we must be grateful for is the knowledge, on the part of all those connected with the program, of just what television is. (© 1971 by The New York Times Company. Reprinted by permission)

We'll look at just a few other examples of how reviewers cope with the medium's peculiarities:

The presentation of political views within a courtroom setting on Public Television's *The Advocates* was contrasted by one reviewer to the dull interview shows broadcast on Sunday afternoons. The purpose in both cases is to examine an issue of importance to the viewer. But unlike the predictable shows on which one "expert" dodges questions from four newsmen, *The Advocates* involves the viewer in a debate that has many of the elements of a Perry Mason showdown. It is an example of lively, inventive news coverage, taking its cue from one of the most successful entertainment formats.

One reviewer, soon after assuming his duties with a daily newspaper, set himself the task of attempting to explain to viewers and producers alike what is wrong (and only very occasionally right) with television choreography. He took every opportunity to educate his audience regarding the odd dimensions of the television screen in contrast to the proscenium opening, the problems associated with flatness and depth created by the video lens, the ponderousness of the studio camera, and the oft-as-not damaging interventions of the director with his special effects gimmickry. When Public Broadcasting carried dance works choreographed and filmed especially for television by Stockholm's Cullberg Ballet, the reviewer lauded the development, explaining how hands are used more expressively and why long runs and giant leaps were rightly omitted to accommodate the confining space of the home screen.

Some dramatic works are more suitable for television than others. Critics praised the video adaptation of Arthur Miller's *The Price* because the tight focus of the TV camera was well suited to capturing the tension between the two brothers as they struggled to impose their opinions upon each other. Conversely, critics have found television adaptations of opera and Broadway plays generally in ignorance of the small screen's requirements. A performance of Benjamin Britten's *Peter Grimes* was largely unintelligible to the uninitiated viewer as a result of excessive long shots that attempted to take in the sweep of a large stage production. "What good is opera as opera on television if the viewer cannot understand what is going on?" one critic lamented.

The following excerpt from a review by Mel Gussow of *The New York Times* examines the adaptation of a live performance to television. Rather than argue for one medium over the other, it attempts to show the strengths and weaknesses of each. The reader gains a better appreciation of both the media and the play—in this case, Jean-Claude Van Itallie's *The Serpent*, as performed by the Open Theater ensemble.

Transferring a performance event to television obviously presents problems, some of them insurmountable. The alternatives are to restage the work entirely or to choose to do only the parts of it that seem readily adaptable to the medium. [Producer Jac] Venze and director Sam Silberman took the second, saner course.

As a result, things are missing. The television 'Serpent' begins with the work's first spoken word, 'Autopsy,' and not, as in a live performance, within the audience with the actors slowly, rhythmically, and musically coming to life. The new beginning is formal, rather than free-flowing.

Gone also is the wildly exuberant after-the-fall, in which apples tumble all over the stage and are gaily bestowed in the audience. The orgy that counterpoints the saying of the 'begats' is now seen in selective, self-censoring closeups. This 'Serpent' loses some of its sensuality and sauciness.

But in certain areas it is enhanced. When I first saw 'The Serpent,' it was in a church. Although the cumulative effect was awesome, in a single viewing, with bad sight lines, one necessarily missed some individual elements. On camera, the line is much clearer. . . . Certain moments . . . are actually heightened in close up.

(© 1970 by The New York Times Company, Reprinted by permission)

Every year the perennial awards ceremonies—Grammy, Tony, Oscar and Emmy—drive the reviewers to distraction: "It was all there—the insipid repartee, the dreary songs, the thank-you-mama speeches, all gloriously capped by Bob Hope at his defensively insulting worst. . . . Hollywood seems gamely determined to keep putting its most pathetic foot forward" (O'Connor, *The New York Times*). So when the Tony Awards show has the good sense to minimize the envelope-opening and maximize the intimate theatrical performances of the stage's brightest stars, the reviews are understandably enthusiastic. Likewise, the beauty pageant that breaks the mold or the holiday parade coverage that finds a fresh format is deservedly praised. All art forms, entertainment vehicles and communications media tend to become ritualistic and ceremonial rather than innovative and imaginative. Television, the most *immediate* medium, suffers worst from this atrophy, and the critic should be the first to call attention to it.

12
Reviews on Television: The 60-second Dash

Broadway legend holds that first-nighters gather with excited antici-pation at Sardi's or some other exclusive restaurant waiting for the obligatory moment shortly after midnight when a publicity flack dashes through the door shouting, "Here they are, hot off the presses: raves in the *Times* and the *Daily News*."

That day, along with Brooks Atkinson, Humphrey Bogart and cars with running boards, is past. Now the producer and his friends sit breathlessly watching television sets, enduring weather maps, sports scoreboards and half a dozen beer commercials until—less than an hour after the final curtain—a dour Edwin Newman takes his cue from the anchor man, stares resolutely at Camera #1, and de-livers a verdict in almost precisely a minute flat. Four reviewers, representing NBC, CBS, ABC and Metromedia, will have called the hit or the miss before the street editions of New York's two morning newspapers appear.

At present, only the largest cities offer enough attractions to war-rant the regular inclusion of reviews in nighttime news programming. But with the spread of cable television in the 1970s and the growth of cultural offerings in the nation's burgeoning population centers, the television review will doubtless become commonplace.

How does the broadcast review differ from the print review?

(1) It has more potential impact.

While the newspaper reviewer is still acknowledged to have the most prestige and the most "power," the broadcast reviewer reaches a larger audience. Print reviews usually appear on the arts and entertainment page, where they are sought out by theatergoers or film buffs. But the broadcast review is part of the news broadcast and is heard by a "captive" audience—many who would not otherwise seek out critical opinions.

While newspaper reading is a solo enterprise, television reviews are frequently heard and watched by a family group, and immediate discussion of the critical appraisal may be generated. One might also argue that, since there is less opportunity for exploration of pro and con nuances, broadcast reviews tend toward a polarity of acceptance or rejection, thus having a more profound effect on the fortunes of the work at hand.

(2) The critic's personality is involved to a greater degree.

Because of journalistic traditions, many print reviewers tend to write essays that sublimate their own personalities. Like news reporters, some avoid writing in the first person. Most print critics can go among the people and not be recognized.

But television is a branch of show business as well as journalism, and the television critic "performs" live. His voice, his facial reactions and his entire image have an important bearing on his review and the way viewers accept it.

WABC-TV in New York pioneered the folksy-chatty newsroom format that turns broadcast newsmen into witty cutups—apparently in an attempt to make the endless bad news cheerful, or at least bearable, to the viewers. As a result, the station's hey-look-at-me critic presents his views in a condescending style riddled with puns, dramatically raised eyebrows and even bantering exchanges with other members of the news staff.

The typical intro for a New York video critic, now that all stations are emulating the successful ABC format, goes:

"Here's Leonard Probst with a review. Len . . ."

"Thank you, Jim . . ."

The reviewer is established as a regular fellow, a trusted buddy. Already he has an advantage over the newspaper reviewer, who has only his by-line and his reputation for an introduction.

The broadcast reviewer's arsenal of weapons, should he decide to pan a play in no uncertain terms, is awesome: scowls, head shakes, thumbs-down hand gestures, gross exaggerations of words for emphasis, and mock incredulity, to name a few of the most popular.

Of course, personality can work both ways. Some of the most thoughtful and intelligent critics appear to be mumbling, colorless dullards when thrust before a camera. One of the Washington, D. C., TV critics has such a huge handlebar moustache and wears such garish bow ties that it takes real discipline to listen to what he's saying. One wonders how influential Clive Barnes would be—tweedy jacket, British accent, gentle lisp and all—if his forum were the TV arena instead of the columns of *The New York Times*.

(3) Time considerations affect the review.

The most profound difference involves the necessary brevity of broadcast reviews. In a half-hour or hour format in which a plane crash gets 35 seconds and a precipitous drop on the stock market warrants no more than 20 seconds, the reviewer is hard pressed to convince the news editor that he really needs much more than a minute of precious air time.

The effect of this necessary brevity is to force the critic into a format—the very outline that a good print reviewer tries to avoid. In the rush at the end, he must merely tick off plaudits—sets, costumes, direction—each with a suitable adjective. Lamenting the time problem, critic Edwin Newman admitted that much Broadway fare isn't worth more than a minute of prime time; it's the occasional exceptional play that gets cheated. In such cases Newman, who has a phenomenal record of hitting the one-minute mark within a few seconds, is occasionally able to convince the news director that he needs an extra half minute.

Producer David Merrick has a particularly low view of television critics: "I loathe each and every one of them. I believe they insult our business with their one-minute reviews. They cannot help us; they can only hurt us. The theater has nothing to gain from them."

The irascible Merrick once personally barred critic Newman from his theater because of another practice brought on by the time pressures of television. Newman made it his policy to attend the final preview before his review. Otherwise it would have been necessary to leave before the final curtain in order to be in the studio on time—and even then the review would have had to be hastily written. Merrick insisted that a preview was like a rehearsal, that opening night was when the cast was "up" for the performance and deserved to be reviewed. Newman countered with two arguments: the price charged for previews (often as high as $10) doesn't suggest that they are merely rehearsals; and the opening night audience is often "stacked" with backers and friends of the producer, resulting in wild

TELEVISION REVIEWS: TIMES AND WORDAGE

A study of television reviews in a one-week period shows an amazing conformity in the length of presentation:

Reviewer*	Type of Review	Time†	Words (approx.)
Probst	Drama	1 minute 8 seconds	200
Klein	Drama	1 minute 14 seconds	180
Newman	Drama	1 minute 1 second	180
Klein	Drama	1 minute 16 seconds	180
Probst	Drama	1 minute 30 seconds	265
Harris	Drama	1 minute 22 seconds	235
Harris	Film	1 minute 20 seconds	195
Harris	Film	1 minute 17 seconds	195
Shalit	Film	1 minute 13 seconds	220
Probst	Drama	1 minute 8 seconds	200
Probst	Drama	1 minute 2 seconds	175
Shalit	Film	1 minute 12 seconds	220
Klein	Film	1 minute 34 seconds	240
Newman	Drama	— 58 seconds	180
Shalit	Film	1 minute 9 seconds	200
Klein	Film	1 minute 18 seconds	220
Average:		1 minute 14 seconds	205

* Leonard Probst, Edwin Newman, Gene Shalit, WNBC-TV; Leonard Harris, WCBS-TV; Stuart Klein, WNEW-TV (Metromedia).
† The uniformity in the rate of words per minute is interesting, considering the apparent wide difference in speaking styles. Shalit's delivery is rapid-fire and clipped, but with pauses between each sentence. Probst reads more slowly but relentlessly. Both average out the same.

applause that can distract the critic from making an accurate assessment. Merrick eventually had to back down.

(4) A "mixed-media" presentation is possible.

Newspaper reviews are frequently illustrated with a single still photograph, and the same device—or a reproduction of a show poster—is possible in television. But the "visuals" can be much more imaginative in TV and may be used to heighten the effect of the review. A head-and-shoulders shot of the critic reading his copy is dull stuff; film clips, readily available from movie press agents, illustrate what the reviewer is saying. A montage of stills from a play can show the costumes and setting while the reviewer uses his limited time to discuss the script and the acting. Dance groups are usually willing to permit television filming of rehearsals so that excerpts can be inserted in the review.

WCBS-TV's Leonard Harris interprets his title, "Arts Editor," to mean that he is not restricted to reviewing. When an internationally famous ballet company comes to town, an intriguing musical goes into production, or an unusual art showing is mounted, he takes a mobile unit and does a feature, sometimes as much as five minutes' worth, including interviews and glimpses of the work in progress. Such features, prepared for showing on the inevitable slow news night, compensate for the limitations of the broadcast review.

(5) It has less "permanence."

One drawback of the television review is that it has life for only a fleeting instant. It cannot be referred to like a newspaper review—unless, of course, it is an unqualified rave, in which case the producer may incorporate all or part of it into his advertising. Newspaper reviews can be clipped, and magazine reviews have a long life. Thus the broadcast review probably tends to help the presold hit rather than the obscure film or drama; it confirms and announces what the public already had reason to expect.

There are two ways of getting around the problem of impermanence. Cyclical radio programming permits repeat broadcasts of a review through the day or an entire weekend. On television, movies and plays can get repeat notices if the arts editor presents a roundup from time to time, especially before holiday periods or weekends.

Clustering related reviews, as Judith Crist does on the *Today* show, can present a helpful comparison of shows competing for attention.

(6) It has far less literary value.

Transcripts of broadcast reviews appear to reveal much less grace and style than one would expect to find in a critical piece. And sometimes the situation is worsened by reviewers who slur words to the point that only the adjectival and noun phrases are heard clearly.

The problem, of course, is that the print review must be constructed in such a way that it reveals 100 percent of its author's purpose and meaning. The script for the television review, on the other hand, is augmented with a "projected attitude" that may show up only as marginal cues or notations. Moreover, in order to avoid a mere reading of the copy, the reviewer tends to ad-lib somewhat, creating nonsentences and engaging in informal delivery.

Consider the following review (Intro: "Here with the review is Edwin Newman. Ed . . ."):

Well, this is one of the more abstruse productions of the season. The Swiss dramatist Durrenmatt has written a takeoff of 'Dance of Death,' one of the last works of the great Swedish dramatist Strindberg. It follows that to get much out of Durrenmatt it helps to be familiar with Strindberg, who has never been much performed in the United States. I happen to have seen 'Dance of Death' fairly recently, and I found the Durrenmatt takeoff amusing. He has burlesqued the Strindbergian war of the sexes, the battle to the death between husband and wife. The trappings suggest a circus, and the play is divided not into scenes, but into rounds, like a prizefight. The cast, Robert Symonds as the husband, Priscilla Pointer as the wife, Conrad Bain as the interloping cousin, gives a controlled performance. That is essential in this kind of enterprise, and the director, Dan Sullivan, must have had a lot to do with it. 'Play Strindberg' is a small thing, but as I said, I found it amusing and it has the additional virtue of being unusual. (WNBC-TV, June 3, 1971)

Drawing meaningful parallels between Strindberg and a "takeoff" on Strindberg in less than 200 words is obviously a task Newman finds impossible. So he delivered a cool, detached and conversational commentary—more "notice" than review. He begins with the relaxed "Well . . ." and doesn't even bother to give the full names of the playwrights mentioned. His summary sentence is personal and low key. The impression is that Newman wished not to insult the intelligence of the five percent of his viewing audience who might be interested in the play, so he merely presented a polite but cursory appraisal and passed out a few kudos.

The *Times* critic, on the other hand, had adequate space (900 words). Thus he could devote four long paragraphs to the concept of one playwright's reworking another's theme. A much fuller synopsis of the action was possible, with a considerable amount of interesting detail concerning the boxing ring staging. And a full sentence's worth of apt and imaginative adjectives and adverbs was devoted to each of the three principals. Even 900 words is insufficient space for a thorough criticism of the work, but Clive Barnes was obviously much more at ease with the task, and his review gave considerable insight into the play.

13
Reaching the
Special Audience

The Big Four in reviews and criticism—Books, Drama, Films and Television—are of interest to the widest possible audience. But there are smaller, special audiences addressed by the mass media who hunger for notices and criticism concerning art and entertainment forms that don't attract quite as large or broad a following.

Dance and classical music lead this secondary field. Also of interest are popular music (concerts and recordings), painting, sculpture, opera, restaurants, architecture, photography and miscellaneous popular attractions such as ice shows and the circus.

Several characteristics of reviewing in these secondary fields should be noted:

(1) The critic is much less likely to make a full-time job out of writing about the field. He may work within the field he reviews, or he may be "moonlighting."

(2) There is a strong tendency for criticism in the secondary fields to be carried in periodic columns rather than in individual reviews. This causes problems of timing and distribution: sometimes there is too much or too little material for the column, or the events have passed by before the review appears.

(3) The writing too often is esoteric and dogmatic. Writing for

a smaller, supposedly well-informed audience leads to assumptions that readers are conversant with special terms and concepts. Part-time reviewers are frequently less aware of the need for explanation and backgrounding in writing for the mass media. And those with sufficient expertise to analyze the fine arts are occasionally merely opinionated rather than critical.

(4) Approaches, attitudes and standards are often not as well formulated, understood or agreed upon. This means that writers in the field must frequently devote part of their space to stating positions or explaining approaches. Whereas the formats and structures of most reviews in the major fields display remarkable similarity, totally different systems may be found in lesser areas.

(5) Protocols and prerogatives are less well defined. Whereas the book reviewer understands the ethics of the "review copy" and the drama critic expects his pair of comps on the aisle, the restaurant critic can't just show up for a free meal—in fact, he probably prefers to work incognito.

(6) The attitude of the editors may be less consistent toward "minority" critics. Editors may vacillate on the amount of preference or "play" assigned to secondary areas, mainly because the editors are less sure of the audience or of the subject matter's importance. Critics working in the major areas are usually deferred to in matters of conflict or overlapping jurisdiction.

In the following sections we shall look at several of the special fields and examine some of their peculiarities.

DANCE

On more than one occasion in the past few years, New York City has been fortunate enough to have two or three major dance companies presenting two- to four-week "seasons" simultaneously. Most evenings, every seat for the overlapping performances was sold. At a time when most of the performing arts are begging for subsidies and patronage, ballet very nearly pays for itself.

The healthy picture of public support doesn't mean that ballet is smugly settled in a groove. As in all performing arts, there is a great deal of tension over which directions to take. In the case of ballet, the choice is between "story" ballet and "abstract," with some critics arguing for a mixture or a blend. Modern dance is arousing much

133

the same argument concerning directions and interpretations; and there are even those who hold that the line between ballet and modern dance is or must be dissolved.

Beyond these arguments over the "state of the art," there are other facets of a dance performance for the critic to focus upon. When a foreign company plays an engagement (or, in other than major cities, when *any* company plays even a one-night stand) the composition of the *corps* and the strengths of the leading dancers might profitably be discussed. The performance of Tchaikovsky's *Eugene Onegin* by the Stuttgart Ballet occasioned this passage by Alan Rich in *New York* magazine:

> The kind of dancing it calls for is actually a sort of highly mobile acting. That is wise, because the company [John] Cranko has built is in good shape to honor such demands. As dancers, in fact, his men aren't very interesting; they seem infinitely more agile in moments of pantomime. Its women are somewhat better: Birgit Keil is, I think, the one ballerina to whom that term really applies; Marcia Haydee is an attractive, sometimes extraordinarily interesting person, but she, too, is more memorable in the dramatic moments than in the purely balletic ones.

Whereas a drama critic calls back for a re-review only as infrequently as there are major cast changes in a long-running plays, the dance critic may attend repeat performances of a single work, perhaps even two in the same day. When a company gears up to do a major story ballet, it may offer a matinee and an evening performance while the bulky scenery is in place. In such cases, the lead roles are often danced by "second-stringers" in the afternoon and by the company's stars in the evening, providing the critic with an opportunity to see two interpretations in the space of a few hours. Russian expatriate Natalia Makarova's Odette-Odile at the evening performance of the American Ballet Theater's *Swan Lake*, contrasted with the same role by another dancer in the afternoon, provides a convincing demonstration of the difference between an exquisite ballerina and a merely competent dancer. Having witnessed the difference, the critic feels justified in the raves he accords Miss Makarova.

Another good reason for paying subsequent visits is to measure the development of the company and its lead dancers as they mature in a production. No two performances are the same, and the hope is that each will exceed the previous as the artists master their technique, develop their roles and grow in their ability to provide nuance.

Many dance companies are virtually artistic dictatorships, with a founding director or choreographer dominating every aspect of the work. This leads to something of an *auteur* theory in dance, with blame and praise for the conception and the execution of a production attributed to the genius of a single man. Paul Taylor is an example of an artist who designs, directs and appears in his own works. His dancers must adopt his particular style of loose-limbed dancing that suits itself to his now-humorous, now-macabre themes.

When the Merce Cunningham production of *Second Hand* appeared to be "less classical" in its second year of performance, Anna Kisselgoff of *The New York Times* found the situation fathomable and explained it to her readers:

Although some of Mr. Cunningham's dances are purposely designed to allow for specific variables in their performance, it is a characteristic of his choreography that even his 'set' pieces can 'look different' from performance to performance. It is a truism by now to point out that Mr. Cunningham is not out to produce movement that will represent a specific emotion. The unpredictability of his movement sequences, based on his belief that any movement can follow another, is bound to produce differing reactions among his viewers.

It is sometimes useful, in the case of classic works performed by a number of companies, to compare the variations in treatment. In recent years, for example, Rudolph Nureyev has rechoreographed and directed a number of ballets, including *The Nutcracker* and *Don Quixote*. As the Associated Press reviewer pointed out: "Nureyev has done what he usually does in adapting, taking out some of the pantomime and adding some dancing, especially for himself. This is all to the good."

While the production of totally new works is considerably less than in some other fields, the dance critic in a major city has an opportunity to evaluate several new items each year. Since innovation has overshadowed revivals and restagings in recent years, the challenge to the critics has been formidable. George Balanchine's New York City Ballet offered a work called *PAMTGG*, based on an airline jingle, and the critics found it trivial at best. Dismissing it as the "nadir" in the choreographer's career, Clive Barnes elaborated in one particularly harsh paragraph:

The choreography reiterated Balanchine's deep commitment to the musical comedy dancing of the 1930s. He seems to have a strange desire to become the Busby Berkeley *de nos jours.* The dancing has an air of nothingness spread thin. It looked like the kind of cabaret routine that can occasionally be seen in the snowbound parts of Switzerland.

As is true of other art forms, dance is taking on new dimensions as it effects courtships and marriages with everything from computers, light shows and kinetic sculpture to films and rock music. The Joffrey Ballet's *Astarte* and Les Grands Ballets Canadiens adaptation of the "rock opera" *Tommy* spurred interest in mixed-media dance programs. The dance critic, like all others, now needs to be much more than merely an expert in one particular field.

Classical music

Programming—the selection and ordering of works to be performed on a given evening—is the initial concern of the music reviewer. The appropriateness of the music is often a key to the performer's success or failure. Here are some examples of programming considerations presented to the reader by the critic in order to put his review in an appropriate and significant setting:

The Juilliard String Quartet is praised for making an effort to include one unfamiliar but major preromantic work in a series of subscription concerts before a college audience.

The Boston Symphony is congratulated for including excerpts from famous ballets in its programs, alongside Bach and Schoenberg. The writer points out that the well-known music is too seldom heard from a full symphony orchestra.

One pianist is criticized for a lack of variety in the first half of his program: one slow Schubert followed another, and the audience lost interest. Another pianist is saluted for fashioning a recital out of transcriptions of pieces originally composed for other instruments and media. The critic salutes the freshness that differentiates this program from "thousands upon thousands of programs almost indistinguishable from one another over the last two decades."

On the occasion of a 70th-birthday salute to Aaron Copland, the critic heartily endorses a selection of the composer's works which accurately sums up his career in just two hours of concert.

Because many readers are unfamiliar with all but the best-known works of the major composers, the critic must turn teacher when evaluating performances of music by lesser-known persons. He may explain that Italian music of the late renaissance was meant to be played in great churches or in sprawling town squares, with groups of musicians opposing one another across vast spaces . . . and that the only adequate performance of the same music today calls for special staging that recreates the antiphonal effect. Or he may instruct his readers in the appreciation of a Bruckner symphony, which demands a certain patience while the orchestra slowly builds tension through repetitions of rhythmic patterns. Or he prefaces his remarks about a flute recital by discussing the literature available for that instrument.

Pulitzer Prize-winning critic Harold Schonberg began one review with a smattering of musical history, explaining that Olivier Messiaen's chamber work was composed while he was in a prison camp during the war, and that he is one of a few composers who sees colors while listening to music—a phenomenon known as synesthesia. Schonberg thought the background important in order to understand the music, which at times is "a curious jumble."

Of prime importance in classical music performance, of course, is the technique of the artist. Inevitably it must be discussed, but with great care, since a string of adjectives describing attack, style, nuance and intonation can quickly degenerate into a meaningless collection of words of no interest to the reader. Ideally, comments on technique are interwoven with a discussion of the concert and summarized at the beginning or the end of the review.

The writer should attempt to make his remarks about technique more than mere textbook references. One critic opened his review with the conjecture that the harpsichordist must have had a plane to catch—notes "sprayed out of his instrument" not only in flashy pieces but also in works that called for a more deliberate approach. The point was made in a lively way, without resorting to a boring lecture on proper harpsichord playing.

In this kind of criticism, too, the critic must assay the development of established artists, indicating whether they are growing, marking time or receding. One pianist is described as "more studied in recent years, with interpretative ideas that come perilously close to affectation." Another, conversely, is lauded because an habitual distortion of phrasing in his early years has yielded to a literal, orthodox interpretation that is infinitely more discreet and musicianlike.

Once again, new works are the real challenge to the music critic.

And, just as in other fields, classical music is undergoing an assault on orthodoxy. The latest symphony of Dimitri Shostakovich, his fourteenth, had the critics puzzling: Is it really a symphony? The work used two solo voices and eleven poems by four poets. Recent symphonic works by other composers have called for taped voices, lighting effects and electronic noises. The critic may decide to take a "wait and see" attitude on a new work if he feels that its true worth might be more apparent after more hearings and an opportunity to discern the direction in which the composer is heading. But the writer may be forced by circumstance to move directly to a defense or condemnation of the work. When a New York audience booed and jeered a piece that included recorded bird calls, the critics pointed to antecedents and asserted the validity of the approach. Conversely, although audiences at the International Society for Contemporary Music concerts in London vigorously supported several innovations, many critics dismissed the "gimmickry" of several of the new works.

Occasionally some consideration other than the program at hand may dominate the critic's review. A concert hall's inaugural concert demands that the writer give precedence to an analysis of the facility's acoustical properties. Until a full orchestra plays in a new hall, nobody knows for certain whether the multimillion-dollar showplace is a hit or a miss. In the autumn of 1971, two new halls were christened on succeeding days. In Washington, the Opera House of the Kennedy Center for the Performing Arts was universally hailed as the best house in America after its gala opening performance. The critics were even willing to overlook garish decor and sloppy workmanship in their exhilaration over the sounds achieved. The next evening, Pittsburgh's new Heinz Hall for the Performing Arts received similar accolades, with much of the tribute going to the German stage designer who consulted with the architects. Beethoven's "Consecration of the House" was dutifully played in Heinz Hall, but a new work specially commissioned for the opening received the main critical attention.

One more area of consideration is the behavior of the audience, never a "constant" at live performances. When *Hair* composer Galt MacDermott's *Mass in F* was premiered in a cathedral, reviewers noted that the overflow audience consisted almost entirely of "nicely dressed, well-mannered and almost solidly white" young people. (*Hair* stressed a biracial theme, the cast bordered on slovenly, and the audience was heavily middle aged.)

And Alan Rich was provoked into devoting one entire week's column in *New York* magazine to a condemnation of the audience's behavior at New York Philharmonic subscription concerts. "What, in the name of God, has happened to good manners and consideration for others?" he demanded, describing the rude babble, the early departures and the inattention. Laying the blame on social climbers who support the symphony because it's the chic thing to do, he proposed:

If I were rebuilding Philharmonic Hall, I think I would add another room, where the patrons could sit comfortably and talk over their week's shopping to a nice background of Muzak, while an audience of the deserving—like the kids who hang around with long faces outside the hall hoping for a ticket—go in to hear the orchestra contribute to our advancement.

OPERA

Many of the points raised in the preceding sections on music and dance also apply to the lyrical stage—observations concerning programming, technique and company strengths or weaknesses, for example. Rather than repeat, let us look at some additional areas of concern to the opera critic—many of which, though first discussed here, apply to a number of the performing arts.

The world opera scene might be described as a few dozen major works and scores of lesser ones, being performed by a few dozen major singers and scores of lesser ones. The leading opera directors strive to bring as many as possible of the top singers—perhaps half a dozen or more in one performance—together in as lavish as possible a production of one of the most venerable works. The resulting under- or overachievement—especially the ability of the major stars to handle the various leading roles—is the concern of the opera critic.

Of most interest to the regular readers of opera reviews is the first performance in a new role by an established singer. When soprano Beverly Sills "dared the lead"—as one writer put it—in Bellini's *Norma*, the director warned her that "a lot of vultures are going to come to hear you sing." The heavily dramatic role was thought

139

to be too stiff a challenge for the light voice of Miss Sills. But she managed to compensate for lack of power with other attributes, and the vultures were disappointed.

Opera buffs are interested in knowing whether a new Rosina in *Il Barbiere di Siviglia* is up to the horseplay that goes with the role, or if a new Violetta in *La Traviata* manages to evoke tragedy, or how a new Lucia handles the Mad Scene. So intense is the cult of personality in opera that the critic cannot go his own way; he must address himself first and foremost to the casting innovations.

For all its intricacies, its demands and its ritually overblown pageantry, grand opera has a strong "the show must go on" tradition. Thus the reviewer not infrequently finds the stage manager stepping out to the footlights to write his lead for him: "Miss Robinson is indisposed; the role of Rosina will be taken by Colette Boky. We beg your indulgence during a short delay of the curtain . . ." The critics discovered at the first intermission of the February 25, 1971, performance at the Metropolitan Opera that Miss Boky had arrived in New York only two hours before curtain time, and that she had never before performed as Rosina. She went on to handle the task more than adequately. The previous night, and also once just a month earlier, two different sopranos had taken falls onstage during performances, injuring themselves. The reviewers found themselves doing considerable straight news reporting as well as opera criticism during those eventful weeks.

Aida is often referred to as "Old Faithful" by critics who find themselves attending Verdi's workhorse extravaganza more often than any other item in the repertory. The traditional double bill of *Pagliacci* and *Cavalleria Rusticana* also sends them into swoons of recognition. But despite the chronic *déjà vu* of opera criticism, enough renewal is constantly going on in most opera companies to keep the writer occupied and challenged. Most companies send one or two works into semiretirement each year so that a few new productions can be introduced into the repertoire each season. Some companies make a practice of opening a new season with a fresh production. Even works that are too popular to be left out of a season must be restaged from time to time, decked out in new costumes and scenery, or perhaps interpreted with fresh emphasis by a director new to the company. On such occasions, singing usually takes second position in the critical appraisal.

There is a tendency, even in the music world, to assume that all worthwhile operas, like antiques, must be at least a century old. Critics, with their eyes toward a full house, must share some of the blame for failing to educate the public to the virtues of new operas. In the 1970–71 season, plaudits were won by an opera based on Tennessee Williams' *Summer and Smoke* and by another based on Mark Twain's *Huckleberry Finn.* Gian-Carlo Menotti, currently the most prolific composer of operas, offered *The Most Important Man,* which explored the agonizing decisions facing a black scientist in racist South Africa. The plight of a childless mother was the theme of Heitor Villa-Lobos' *Yerma,* originally written in English for an all-black cast but performed initially in Spanish. Two of the four new works were performed in New York, one in St. Paul and another in Santa Fe. Opera *is* alive and well and living wherever critics help create a favorable climate for it.

There is a danger that new works will fade after their premieres, losing out to the old standby Puccinis and Verdis. *La Boheme* is virtually synonymous with Puccini, yet there is a perfectly enjoyable version of the same tale by Leoncavallo which deserves attention. Benjamin Britten's *Billy Budd,* an interesting novelty because of its all-male cast, is seldom played, despite the audience's familiarity with the Melville story.

How can a critic prod producers and audiences to take an occasional look into the neglected treasury? By taking every opportunity to remind them of what they are missing—by suggesting in his *La Traviata* notice, for example, that instead of having *La Traviata* in everybody's repertoire year after year each company should vow to resuscitate one "oldy-but-goody" each season, showing its dedication to living (versus fossilized) opera. And also by going overboard to write at length about the new and the forgotten works when they manage to surface from time to time. Not just a single notice, but a feature . . . a Sunday column as well . . . perhaps even a magazine article.

PAINTING, SCULPTURE AND PHOTOGRAPHY

Grouping these three major art forms in no way implies that they are less important than other areas. But the trio are often gathered under one roof and handled by one critic. As the scope of our museums increases, the lines between the various media are increasingly blurred.

The art critic rarely addresses himself to a single work. He is usually concerned with an artist who is represented in a gallery showing or museum retrospective, or he must evaluate a museum exhibition covering a group of artists, a period or a movement.

In attempting to describe the work of a new artist, the writer may focus on one representative work or he may better be able to give a "feel" for the artist's style by citing elements common to all of the works on display. The showing of an established artist or group is approached with another set of questions in mind: Why did the museum director feel this body of material was relevant? What does the show represent? Is the show balanced? Does the show have a point of view, and how well does it come across? Or is the show instructive, and if so are the examples valid? Along the same line, how does the current show relate to the overall objectives of the institution? And, of course, is the exhibition presented pleasingly?

In attempting to answer these questions, fidelity to art form is important, but responsibility to audience is every bit as crucial. An ambitious bringing together of two hundred cubist works may be criticized for overwhelming the museumgoer, subjecting him to dozens of inferior works instead of helping him to comprehend the development of an approach to art as seen through important major works. Leading art critic John Canaday scored a display of computer art because the "explanatory" labels accompanying the works were intelligible only to those versed in computer language.

Many showings lend themselves to feature news coverage as well as, or even better than, straight critical review. Kinetic sculpture, "happenings" and mixed-media shows cry out for television coverage. Newpapers can get interesting interviews with the young artists who erect 60-foot pylons in museum courtyards or spend two days suspending hundreds of feet of twisted neon tubing from the ceiling of an exhibition hall. It's up to the art critic to keep the news desk informed about feature possibilities.

Many major museums have mounted shows in recent years reflecting the ideas that "cultural milieu" is one of their legitimate concerns and that "art's reflection of social change" is a valid theme for an exhibition. "Harlem on My Mind," "Puerto Ricans—Here and There" and "City of Promise: Jewish Life in New York, 1654–1970" used photographs, art and artifacts, specially commissioned book catalogs, and new educational techniques such as tape-cassette commentary to add dimension to the art museum concept. "Another Chance for Cities" was underwritten by the New York State Urban Development Corporation, which commissioned architects and planners to visualize the city of the future.

The touring city exhibition attracted news coverage as well as critical attention when it appeared in various art museums. Similarly, the Harlem and Puerto Rico shows were written about by blacks and Puerto Ricans on the feature pages and in the minority media. Art critics, thankfully, no longer have the art world all to themselves.

ARCHITECTURE

Ask an editor—or one of his readers—to list "all the kinds of critics you can think of," and chances are architecture won't occur to him. This despite the fact that the first Pulitzer Prize for criticism went to architecture critic Ada Louise Huxtable.

The face of America was drastically altered in the booming Sixties; the "renewal" of our center cities was one of our most important tasks. The job was entirely in the hands of businessmen, planners, legislators, chambers of commerce, and large firms of architects which ground out plans for massive boxes of concrete or glass-walled steel. The few small voices of the architecture critics were drowned out by the spirited bidding of construction contractors. There has been no greater shame since Mussolini blotted the landscape of suburban Rome with his sterile chunks of granite.

Architecture is the enclosing of space for man's use, in harmony with nature and surrounding objects. An architect does not merely "design a building," he makes an addition to or an alteration of an environment. The critic of architecture, then, must be privy to the earliest plans for change, so that he might call attention to faulty planning. He should not wait until he is confronted with a completed structure. Nor should he base his earliest comments merely on a drawing or a balsa model of the individual building. Instead, he must endeavor to understand the heritage of an entire city or neighborhood, the character and the needs of the people who live there, and the master plan for the development and improvement of the entire area. Only then can he judge the appropriateness of the specific design for an individual structure. When a new civic building rose from the earth in a cleared section of Boston's downtown area, some citizens were horrified by the "strange, modern" structure. Architecture writers, using drawings and photographs of the building and its surrounding neighbors, demonstrated how the structure reflected and complimented the other facades, continuing their lines in a fresh way, contrasting or harmonizing interestingly in terms of color and texture. The "strange" new edifice was actually well suited to the location—once one was able to comprehend the larger view.

Ada Louise Huxtable was particularly critical of the $66-million Kennedy Center for the Performing Arts which opened in Washington, D. C., during the summer of 1971:

> Because it is a national landmark, there is only one way to judge the Kennedy Center—against the established standard of progressive and innovative excellence in architectural design that this country is known and admired for internationally.
> Unfortunately . . . what it has in size, it lacks in distinction. Its character is aggrandized posh. It is an embarrassment to have it stand as a symbol of American artistic achievement before the nation and the world.
> The Kennedy Center not only does not achieve this standard of innovative excellence; it did not seek it. The architect opted for something ambiguously called 'timelessness' and produced meaninglessness. . . .

She found herself compelled to admit that her fellow citizens strolling through the building in their T-shirts, hot pants and sneakers appeared to feel perfectly at home in "a safe, familiar blend of theatrical glamour and showroom Castro Convertible."

If there are too few architecture critics, there is ample opportunity for other writers to exercise the function when new facilities are unveiled within their realms. As mentioned earlier, music critics must judge the acoustics and other properties of a new concert hall. When the new Walker Art Center opened in Minneapolis, art critic Hilton Kramer devoted the first half of his "premiere showing" review to the "starkly minimalist" building itself:

> I suspect it is going to be one of those buildings that will change a lot of minds about what we can and should expect from the architects who design our new museums. For here, amazingly enough, is a new museum building that gives cheerful priority to the works of art it is meant to house.

FOOD AND RESTAURANTS

Egad! Howard Johnson's fried clams considered in the same volume with Pinter and Puccini? Well, not quite. But *Les Sylphides* and *les escargots* are equally serious matters among connoisseurs, and critics of haute cuisine are having their day in the mass media.

What *Dance* magazine and *Opera News* are to their particular constituencies, *Gourmet*, "the magazine of good living," and the West Coast's *Sunset* magazine are to aspiring chefs. *Gourmet*'s "Paris à Table" column reviews two or three leading French restaurants each month, and "Spécialités de la Maison" discusses the merits of New York's leading eating establishments. Preeminent among the travel magazine restaurant and food writers is *Travel & Leisure*'s Myra Waldo, who also reviews restaurants for radio and is the author of several travel and eating guides. New York City's theater magazines—*Playbill*, *Playfare* and *Cue*—regularly include restaurant reviews, reflecting the important interrelationship of playgoing and dining out in America's entertainment capital.

As in so many other fields, the restaurant critic (who carries the prosaic title of "food editor") of *The New York Times* is one of the most influential in a city renowned for its French and Italian restaurants, Jewish delicatessens and varied Chinese cuisine. For many years, Mississippi-born Craig Claiborne rated Gotham's finest from four stars to none, chiding a posh restaurant for using too much lemon in a sauce, serving "gross" portions, or diminishing the *ambiance* (a word Claiborne popularized) by squeezing the tables too close together. His *Dining Out in New York* not only provides a guide to the leading restaurants of the city, it is virtually a short course in how to fully enjoy a first-class repast.

When Claiborne retired, he was succeeded by Raymond A. Sokolov, who added another index to the weekly review column— four triangles to none—rating service, atmosphere and decor. Sokolov's first review introduced his readers to an obscure Chinese restaurant forty-five miles south of the city on historic U. S. Route 1, near Princeton, N. J. As a result, reservations a week in advance are now necessary at A Kitchen, and the proprietor is planning to move into larger quarters to handle the additional business.

The restaurant critic obviously must be familiar with the world's great cuisines, most notably French, Italian and Chinese (French and Italian are sometimes lumped together under the heading of "continental"). Most are good cooks themselves—they have to be in order to know just what misstep makes the hollandaise separate.

In recent years, two publications have blazed new trails in food writing, going beyond the mere "restaurant rating" column found in many newspapers and magazines.

One is *New York* magazine, which explains the art of dining in three different columns. Gael Greene's "Restaurants" column focuses on the elegant eating spots, frequently stripping away the pomposity and snobbishness that intimidates diners who would like to try The Four Seasons despite the fact that they aren't listed in the social register. "The Underground Gourmet" by Milton Glaser and Jerome Snyder rates less expensive establishments on four criteria: food, service, ambiance and hygiene. Various staff members prepare reports for "The Passionate Shopper," a column which instructs budding chefs on how to save money while obtaining good wines and ingredients for gourmet cooking.

The Minneapolis *Star*'s "Taste" section, appearing once a week concurrently with heavy foodstore advertising, provides another example of innovative food coverage. Realizing that their readership was ready and eager for more than just the usual bland recipes and "hints," the editors appointed Beverly Kees—a young woman with experience in women's news, general reporting and the business page—to supervise the 16- to 24-page section. She has visited New York, San Francisco and cities in France in a quest for fresh ideas, and she draws on other staff writers who are interested in haute cuisine for columns and articles. Her section begins with full-page color graphics tied to the lead article or the week's theme. The newspaper gives the section heavy promotion, and reader response is encouraging. Most important of all, the department is completely separate from the women's and society pages—the staff members involved consider "Taste" to be related as closely to "Arts, Leisure and Entertainment" as to any other area of interest.

Popular live entertainment

What can you say about "The Greatest Show on Earth" or that schmaltzy crowd-pleaser, the ice revue?

Not much bad, unless you want to win the Scrooge award for mean, nasty criticism. To be sure, the circus came in for some hard knocks in the late 1950s when it began to look like a tacky second-rate version of televised entertainment; and some critics deplored Peggy Fleming's overly "packaged and produced" act in her first appearance with Holiday on Ice. But, by and large, reviewing the popular extravaganzas means taking the kids along, glutting yourself on peanuts or candy floss, and composing a valentine that describes rather than evaluates.

When Peggy Lee plays the Persian Room, Joan Baez fills Carnegie, or the ever-popular Victor Borge packs 'em in from Atlanta to Seattle, the critics may decide that the better part of valor dictates a sublimation of comments about technical flaws or repetitive programming. There must be a limit to ritual adoration, however. When the 1970 contingent of the Vienna Boys Choir included a playlet version of Humperdinck's *Hansel and Gretel* in their repertoire, the critics observed that the weakness of some voices and the Sunday School mannerisms of the ensemble did not do justice to the operatic work.

RECORDINGS

Now that a record album—*Jesus Christ Superstar*—has been made into a Broadway show, instead of the other way around, editors may stop relegating record news to the space left over under the philately column. Except for an occasional bow to a new Beatles album, the mass media left the job of serious record/tape reviews to the specialized media during the 1960s.

The problem is that record reviews in the special audience papers and magazines are often incomprehensible to all but the most ardent devotees of a musical group: only if you have already committed Bob Dylan's newest album to memory can you comprehend what the reviewer is saying, because the reviewer is so "into" the cuts that he's rendered inarticulate.

The Calendar section of the Sunday *Times* in Los Angeles offers its readers a popular record column that attempts to give an adequate description and evaluation of each album for a general audience. *Saturday Review* considers classical recordings in its frequent multimedia section and provides an annual roundup of worthy additions to the

147

classical library. The best attempt to present useful, easily understood analyses of both popular and classical recordings was to be found in *Show* magazine, which has appeared sporadically.

Reviewing John Lennon's personal album, *John Lennon/Plastic Ono Band*, Robert Hilburn of the *Los Angeles Times* did the kind of thorough reportorial and analytical job that may one day raise record reviewing to equal status with drama and literary criticism. He compared and contrasted the album with current ones by the other former Beatles and by Bob Dylan. He interviewed Lennon confidant Dr. Arthur Janov, author of *The Primal Scream*, and he related material on the record to comments about Lennon in Hunter Davies' authorized biography of the Beatles. In the second half of the 1500-word review he reproduced lyrics from three songs to illustrate the points he was making. By the time Hilburn came to his conclusion that Lennon's album is a remarkable achievement, he had adequately and interestingly documented the opinion.

14
Comparing
and Contrasting

"Whatever Judith Crist likes, I usually like. So she's the only critic
I read . . ."

If culture functioned as toasters and waffle irons do, *Consumer
Reports*, with its panel of testers, could take over the critic's job.
But, as we have seen, the intelligent reader expects to find much more
than consumer advice in the mass media reviews. Studies show that
audience members who "seek out" reviews (as opposed to "coming
across" them) in the mass media tend to seek out more than one
review, in order to make a comparison. One study indicated that
this was because of a reluctance to "take the word of one critic"—
quite the opposite of the individual who trusts Judith Crist without
question.

Certainly the would-be critic profits from comparing and contrasting several reviews of the same work. And so, in the following pages,
key segments of related reviews will be juxtaposed in order to evaluate and appreciate the approaches of various writers. As a structure
for our analysis, we shall consider a single, limited aspect of each
group of reviews, excerpting the lines or paragraphs which speak
to the issue.

Two by Two—KAYE'S CONTRIBUTION

Richard Rodgers was one magic name associated with the musical comedy *Two by Two*, and Danny Kaye was the other. When all the reviews were in, Mr. Rodgers got a polite nod for one or two hummable numbers, while Kaye garnered the lion's share of the honors. The musical, based on *The Flowering Peach* by Clifford Odets, was poorly received by the majority of the critics. They labeled it cutely sentimental, overly long, coarse, stale and even pointless. With those evaluations, only bravura could save the play. According to a sufficient number of critics, that is just what Kaye provided.

(Clive Barnes, *New York Times*) Danny Kaye is a great and a good man, and last night at the Imperial Theater he returned to the Broadway stage after an absence of nearly 30 years. You had better go and see him now, because at this rate he won't be back until 1999. And even though he then might possibly be in a better play, is it really worth the wait? Mr. Kaye is so warm and lovable an entertainer, such a totally ingratiating actor, that for me at least he can do no wrong . . . it is Mr. Kaye's show. Fighting a deplorable sound system, which made his voice come more from the side of the stage than out of his mouth, Mr. Kaye was a continual and continuous delight as the 600-year-old Noah. The man's energy is amazing. He sings, he dances. On one occasion he even piercingly whistles and succeeds in keeping the show pushing on. And when he has some of Mr. Rodgers' best numbers to sing, everything comes together and the show glows.

(Richard Watts, *New York Post*) Mr. Kaye is altogether brilliant in the demanding part, making *Two by Two* worth seeing if only for his memorable performance. Whether he's playing the eminent builder of the ark at an advanced age or as the temporary possessor of the youth the Old Testament God bestowed upon him, whether he is being serious or humorous, acting Mr. Stone's book or singing Mr. Rodgers' songs, he is the truly great performer he has always been.

(Ernest Albrecht, *Home News*) Danny Kaye first appears as a decrepit man, 600 years old. The delightful clown is submerged beneath a rickety walk, a tummy, grumpiness and a shedding flaxen wig. But after a few moments Kaye rubs his weary back along a post, and a sly smile creeps across his toothless mouth and suddenly we can see the Kaye we know and love. His smile is something of a secret. It knows something very funny, but dares not laugh out loud without being downright silly. But the smile spreads, the jaw gains strength, the body vigor. Kaye goes offstage to allow one of God's and the theater's miracles to take place and becomes 90 again. It is a magical moment, one Rodgers' music and the lyrics of Martin Charnin capture, allowing Kaye to expand, to raise his almost musical voice and rejoice over his new found youth. We can rejoice, too, for from now on Kaye can be himself. From that moment on the show is a delight, with Kaye cavorting, manipulating, managing the whole affair with that incredibly private smile that paradoxically makes mirth so public . . . Kaye must exert his own personality on the show. Without his personal appeal, the second half of the show would be very limp indeed. But Kaye is there, so why quibble? He keeps the sun shining during all the 40 days and nights of gloomy weather and the soggy aftermath.

(T. E. Kalem, *Time*) That leaves Danny Kaye with rather more than he can salvage. Kaye is not naturally funny but more of a stuntman of humor who relies on glib footwork, a glibber tongue and a foxy attitude for facial contortions. He has had to subdue these in *Two by Two* and concentrate on just being liked. He works long and arduously at it, and he is liked. And pitied. At show's end he is supposed to be 601 years old, and few in the opening-night audience felt appreciably younger.

(Jack Kroll, *Newsweek*) Great git-gat-giddle, can Danny Kaye be an institution? Well, this show has at least temporarily institutionalized him, and he gives every sign of being damned sore about that. Kaye is of course one of the greatest of all *tummlers*, those frenetic, wild-eyed, swift-sneakered boys, largely Jewish, whose job it was to create relentlessly gay activity—tumult—among the guests at the great hotels on the Borscht Circuit. Kaye did this with genius, bouncing like a kosher Petrouchka through the '40s with his romantic blond hair, his moonstruck stare, his mad giggle, his chameleon tongue that could lick the polysyllables from a bowl of alphabet soup at ten paces. *Two by Two* treats Danny very badly . . . Kaye is given such cretinous old-man things to do and say that when he is temporarily made young again midway in the first act he leaps joyfully onstage as if he's just paid a sneakily satisfactory visit to the outhouse. . . . And director-choreographer Joe Layton's silly schlep-steps manage to make even Kaye look bad.

(Henry Hewes, *Saturday Review*) Oddly enough, the musical virtually reduces that unique performer, Danny Kaye, into a character actor. For a brief moment near the beginning when God's response to Noah's questions are indicated by David Hays's quick succession of projected images of familiar paintings by artists ranging from Michelangelo to Van Gogh, there is a sense of style. But this style cannot be sustained, and Kaye

151

must revert to the plot and the dreary domestic problems of Noah's household. Although he does this adequately, he is not as effective as was the late Menasha Skulnik, who played the role originally, for the simple reason that his stage personality is not as well suited to the part. Indeed, the star's most effective moment comes when he turns up miraculously rejuvenated and struts about like a proud and sexy rooster. Here we are led to hope that Danny's himself again and that he will go on to overwhelm us with the things he does best. But it does not happen. The show simply neglects to create Danny Kaye's special world.

(Brendan Gill, *The New Yorker*) I mean to say as little as possible about *Two by Two*, at the Imperial, because my chief feeling in regard to it is one of sadness. It is as nearly dead as a musical can be, and Danny Kaye's attempt to make his own superb vitality mask the lack of it in the book, music and lyrics is heroic and in vain.

(John Simon, *New York*) This semirecumbent mixture, however, gets a leavening from the mostly delightful performances. Danny Kaye just about redeems himself from his appalling rendition of the Ragpicker in the movie *Madwoman of Chaillot*. Here he is essentially restrained, even dignified, flavorous and funny enough when called for, but, above all, quite likable. And that is a very nice thing to have in the middle of a brassy musical.

(Jack Richardson, *Commentary*) There has always been a mystique about Danny Kaye that has baffled me. Some very intelligent people have found him a master of comedy, a perfect embodiment of aerial whimsy. On the other hand, I have always considered him a gross, obtrusive performer who begged for his laughs by mugging, bodily exaggerations, nonsense sounds, and other similarly infantile devices. However, I had never seen Kaye on the stage, so I went to *Two by Two* hoping to be disabused of the bad impression of him that I had culled from the movies and television. What took place on the stage of the Imperial Theater proved that I had been too generous in my evaluation. If anything, this retelling of the legend of Noah, his ark, and the divine inundation made Kaye seem more outlandishly grotesque than ever before. It is one thing to wink and wiggle through a performance of *The Kid From Brooklyn;* but to bring those attributes to the portrayal of a patriarch and agent of God goes beyond poor performing into blasphemous self-indulgence.

Summary: Most of the critics appear to have been predisposed to like or dislike Danny Kaye. His detractors specifically named past sins for which they held him responsible, while his admirers spoke in general terms, assuming, apparently, that Kaye could hardly do any wrong. Only one writer contrasted his performance to that of an earlier Noah.

The two reviews that say the least—about Kaye, or about the play—seem to imply that it was someone else's fault, not Kaye's. Two reviewers found the star a delight, two labeled him likable. Six of the nine reviewers made the section on Kaye the focal point of their review; the other three subordinated any mention of Kaye to a general attack on the play's inappropriateness. The favorable majority were borne out: the play enjoyed a season's run, trading almost entirely on the indomitable Danny Kaye—even when he injured his foot and was forced to perform from a wheelchair.

Orlando Furioso: INVOLVING THE AUDIENCE

"Theater in the surround" is what Luca Ronconi of the Teatro Libero di Roma called his production of *Orlando Furioso,* based on Ariosto's 16th-century epic poem. The show, a big hit in Spoleto, Italy, and elsewhere in Europe, was staged under a huge plastic bubble in Bryant Park behind the New York Public Library. The audience milled around in the open area between two stages, frequently having to dodge actors on trollies who moved rapidly from one stage to the other, sometimes setting up impromptu acting areas en route. The critic for *The Wall Street Journal* summed it up as "a dazzling entertainment for everybody, a mixture of carnival, Fellini, circus, tournament, commedia dell'arte, Anna Magnani and the bustling streets of Rome."

The critics were definitely divided, which led to a series of advertisements featuring two sets of excerpts: "They didn't get it" and "They did." The city, which had sponsored the show, hoped to get at least a lively dialog going about the unusual theatrical event, and incidentally to boost attendance.

Most of the reviewers agreed that *Orlando Furioso* was theater, or at least a theatrical event. But they split over the question of whether or not the audience was really involved. Were they genuinely swept up in the spirit and eventually synthesized into the action? Or were they somewhat baffled, merely tolerant, and perhaps even put off by the swirling horseplay around them?

(Mel Gussow, *New York Times*) The story is almost impossible to follow, and not much fun when you find your place. . . . After about 90 nonstop minutes, immediately following the Battle of Paris, Orlando finally discovers his long-lost love, Angelica. But she is now in love with a lowly Saracen. This drives Orlando furioso. He's not the only one.

(Clive Barnes, *New York Times*) . . . the show is highly enjoyable for 10 minutes, pleasant enough if you have friends in the audience you can chat with, for at base it is more of a social than theatrical occasion, and oddly just as satisfying to read about as actually to see. Theater as a social happening may have possibilities, especially in villages such as Spoleto, where 'Orlando' started, and Manhattan's dramatic precinct. . . . Admittedly, people who speak a little Italian will presumably get more out of it than people who don't, but it is not a play with a text. It is surely intended as a theatrical occurrence evoking responses more to do with form and style than with content.

(Jack Kroll, *Newsweek*) . . . the seatless audience mills, gapes and marvels. The audience is part of the show as a dreamer is part of his dream, startled by and evading the eruptions of fantastic, juggernauting events and creatures that appear out of nowhere. . . . The dialogue is Italian, of course, but the excellent program makes everything clear, and a mummy could follow the vehement emotions projected by the spirited troupe. . . . 'Orlando' has forced spectators to show the same sharp reflexes in the face of fresh, primal feeling and unequivocal energy as they habitually do in the face of oncoming automobiles, lurching drunks, pouncing muggers and the sneaky miasma of urban anxiety. The experience is bracing and delightful, and Ronconi is obviously one of the most imaginative men in world theater.

(Brendan Gill, *The New Yorker*) I've never read a word of this masterpiece, and I suspect I never will, but my ignorance of the original didn't keep me from having a marvellous time at a dramatized enactment of the poem. . . . The spectacle resembles nothing so much as a manic, or perhaps even demonic, Wild West show in a Renaissance setting, and I think you will find it incomprehensible and exhilarating, and well worth a visit.

(John Lahr, *The Village Voice*) Epic, gigantic, operatic, outrageous—it is like walking into your most heroic dream, awake. . . . For the audience as well as the knights errant, it is every man for himself. Theatre becomes sport. The audience, themselves transformed into a new community of seekers, rushes to meet the action wherever the stories unfold around them. They learn quickly how to dodge the dangerous 20-foot steel horses caroming around the floor. Caught up in the festival spirit of the event, they hiss the villians and bravo the flamboyant passion of the actors with their posturing and rolled "r's." I have never seen anything like it. . . . Because most of the audience cannot fall back on English to make sense of the production's myriad plot lines, they must either enter into the vectors of action or walk away as disgruntled at real play as they are at real life. Experiencing *Orlando Furioso* is like finding the meaning of a Pollock painting: you must accept it, find a place to begin, then follow the energy. . . . Teatro Libero guides the audience gently and in good humor, not in one but many directions. The audience makes up its own event, by discovering it; steered by the busy performers who frame them and vie with such humor and guile for their attention . . . the actors leave. What is left of this fabulous event is the audience groping through the chicken-wire labyrinth looking for the next piece of the spectacle. . . . *They* are looking at each other, actors in their own drama.

(John Simon, *New York*) In this theater, in the *actual* midst, we can do nothing but run or be run over. We cannot follow the plot or prosody—even if we know the story and the language—because it moves too fast and is scattered all over. . . . As John Lahr, that particularly rabid beater of wooden drums for the avant-garde, wrote in his *Village Voice* column, this *Orlando* allows us 'to see . . . primal theatrical energy,' to be 'staring performing energy in the eye.' And he upbraids our culture 'which likes to keep things "normal" . . . and puts its "psychotics" out of sight.' 'Emotion,' laments Lahr, 'is kept at a safe distance.' Hogwash. Art is never raw energy to be stared in the eye (a single eye, it seems, like the raging Cyclops'), but is the molding, shaping, channeling, controlling of energy. 'Primal theatrical energy' is in the mind of a Shakespeare, Chekhov or Beckett, and no one can stare it in the eye or beat it out with wooden swords against tin horses. And if this kind of audience participation exercises the legs, it unhappily bypasses the brain. As for our society, I don't see it keeping many things normal these days, or emotion at a distance. And where would Lahr have us put our psychotics? Into the drama reviewer's seat, no doubt.

(Harold Clurman, *The Nation*) We are, in effect, strollers at a street fair, looking at whatever pleases us most at the moment. I found myself spinning around so I would miss nothing. . . . It is not however a show for the aged and sedentary. It cannot be appreciated in the complacent mood of a person down front, goggling at a Broadway musical.

(Richard Watts, *New York Post*) An extravagant claim has been made for this 'Orlando' which I must combat. 'No audience,' it goes, 'could experience a performance and then be content to sit in the tenth row center of any play produced and feel actively involved in a theatrical adventure. This production has opened the doors to a new standard of communication.' Personally, I would be more content to sit in the 15th row far on one side at a play on a stage, where I wouldn't have to keep ducking platforms, and I would derive more emotional satisfaction from it.

155

Summary: At one extreme stood John Lahr, a young critic who shows his disdain for typical Broadway fare by attending opening nights in casual garb. Not surprisingly, the acerbic John Simon took him to task. At the opposite extreme was the kindly traditionalist Richard Watts, who obviously likes the warm comfort of a red velvet Shubert chair. The division over this show paralleled reactions to other "audience participation" theatrical events. A year later, however, some reviewers who had been cool to *Orlando Furioso* professed to enjoy the tactile fun-and-games atmosphere of The James Joyce Memorial Liquid Theatre. Over a period of two or three years, audiences learned to loosen up and meet the actors at least part way.

Simon, lone among the dissenters, speaks to the issue in terms of the question "What is art?" The others react purely in an impressionistic way, voicing their personal discomfort. The majority of the supporters, too, were heavily impressionistic in their approach. Only Lahr and Simon, on the two extremes, really went deeply into psychological reaction. Perhaps the reason most critics avoided the more "pretentious" approach was that the carnival atmosphere of the "extravaganza under the bubble" just didn't seem to merit it.

Hamlet: TO BE, OR NOT TO BE, INTERESTED ANEW

"The memory be green . . ." goes a line early in *Hamlet*. And so it is for the reviewer who confronts one melancholy Dane hard upon the heels of another. Within a three-month period, Mel Gussow, backup reviewer for *The New York Times*, was confronted by four productions of Shakespeare's masterpiece. The only thing that made the marathon tolerable for Gussow was the fact that three of the productions were rather unorthodox. The following excerpts—in each case the lead paragraph—indicate what was novel about each production.

(1) The idea of using male actors in female roles is at least as old as Shakespeare, which entitles director Gene Feist to call his all-male *Hamlet* an Elizabethan production. Unlike *As You Like It*, which Britain's National Theater staged all-male in 1968, *Hamlet* is not concerned with the confusion of the sexes. But one of its concerns is sex, and as produced by the Roundabout Theater, where it opened last night, it is stripped of its sexuality. Thankfully, this is not a sensationalized, sniggery *Hamlet*, but it is largely a cold one.

156

(2) I had forgotten what an uncut *Hamlet* was like until I visited the CSC Repertory Theater. But there it is—down to the most minor courtier, and the last flutter of Osric's hat. Certainly the CSC is to be congratulated for the attempt. But although the company is a good one—most of the leads are well cast—it is not good enough to compel one's interest for three and one half hours.

(3) In *Beyond the Fringe*, Jonathan Miller and his comic partners did a hilarious takeoff on Shakespeare. Miller is still mocking the Bard. His latest prank is his Oxford & Cambridge Shakespeare Company production of *Hamlet*, which began a limited run Saturday night at the Hunter College Playhouse. This time, however, the joke is really on Miller. Miller's *Hamlet*, not to be confused with Shakespeare's *Hamlet*, is stubbornly contrary, like the March Hare. It is not so much a conception as an arbitrary assault. Almost everything is done differently, just to be different, a maneuver that leads the director into a series of collisions with his author.

(4) Dame Judith Anderson has had a long, distinguished career in the theater and for some time has dreamed about playing *Hamlet*. Not just in *Hamlet*—after all, she once was Gertrude to Gielgud's Hamlet—but as Hamlet. Madness? Folly? Disaster? Before Miss Anderson played her *Hamlet* at Carnegie Hall last night one expected a little bit of everything. Should any 72-year-old lady attempt to play Hamlet? Not this 72-year-old lady. It is really not a question of her sex—ladies have played *Hamlet* before—or of her age, although as with actors who grow old gracefully, she might have settled for Lear or Falstaff. It is not the simple absurdity of the casting, but it is a question of her acting. She has no concept, no consistent approach, and apparently director William Ball has none, either—except perhaps to emasculate *Hamlet*. This is a bloodless production, with no power, poetry, or humor.

Summary: Sexual reality and fidelity to the original are the recurring themes of Gussow's repeat visits to the classic. He does not appear to have tired of attempts to approach *Hamlet* in new ways; each production is approached without prejudice and granted its attempt at innovation. He does not belabor the reader with a course in Shakespearean drama, assuming familiarity on the part of the audience. In all four reviews, the balance of the space was devoted to a discussion of the various actors and how they handled their roles.
If anything, the sum attitude reflected in this group of reviews is that the critic is patiently marking time, waiting for a truly worthy and exciting production of *Hamlet* to come along—perhaps the equivalent of Nichol Williamson's performance a few years back—

quite aware that for every great Dane there must be a whole litter
of whimpering puppies.

The Go-Between: WHICH ELEMENT TO FEATURE?

The Go-Between, at once a simple and complex motion picture to
write about, received unanimous raves when it opened in this country
a few months after winning the grand prize at the Cannes film festival. The critics differed not in their opinions of the picture but in
their choice of an element around which to build the review. So
uniformly laudatory were the reviews that Columbia Pictures assembled photocopies of all the notices printed in New York papers and
took advertisements offering the collection to any reader who re-
quested them. Here are the lead paragraphs (followed by an indication of the structure of the balance of each review):

(Vincent Canby, *New York Times*) When Leo Colston, who will be
13 on the 27th, goes to visit his classmate at Brandon Hall in July of
1900, the elegant Mandsley family receives him with that special gracious-
ness reserved for poor but well-bred boys, the sort who live with
widowed mothers in small neat cottages, far enough away so as not to
be social embarrassments. (Three more paragraphs about plot and setting
followed; at the midpoint of the review, Canby explained that it is not
the boy's story that commands attention "but the picture of the golden
society through which the boy moves, and the beautifully defined am-
biguity of the relationships of the adults that tower above him." Stars,
writer and director were accorded one-sentence comments. Then a long
paragraph explained how the movie camera and the editing provide a
"complex, contradictory kind of revelation." The Cannes prize was mentioned in the final paragraph.)

(Wanda Hale, *New York News*) As a rule the Cannes Film Festival ·
Grand Prix awards cut no ice with me. I've seen too many of the arbitrary
selections by the grandpappy of all film festivals to hold my breath
until they get here. This year the voters are to be congratulated for
giving the top award to an English production, not anti-anything, to
Joseph Losey-Harold Pinter's *The Go-Between.* (Then came four paragraphs about the writing and filming, two paragraphs about plot, and
five paragraphs about the actors. The *News* assigned its top four-star
rating to the picture.)

(Archer Winsten, *New York Post*) *The Go-Between,* at the 68th St.
Playhouse, sporting its top prize from Cannes, its screenplay by Harold
Pinter himself, its direction by that American hairshirt of British aris-

tocracy, Joseph Losey, displays a tender appreciation of the beauties and niceties of the great stately homes of England when they were in their prime. For a good long while one feels no denigration at all of the aristocrats and their vistaed lawns, their deer herd of antlered bucks and does, their silver and servants, and their son's visiting friend young Leo (Dominic Guard). (The remaining four paragraphs included interwoven comments about actors, technique and the film's overall effect.)

(John Broeck, *The Villager*) Joseph Losey, an American director expatriated to Britain, makes his most profound films in collaboration with Harold Pinter. Many would rate *The Servant* and *Accident* high on the list of best films ever. Their latest work, *The Go-Between*, is about as close to perfection in films as one will ever get. (Pinter's playwrighting style was discussed first, then story and actors together.)

(Steven Kohn, *Gramercy Herald*) [On the other hand] we have the delicate yet penetrating beauty of Joseph Losey's *The Go-Between* which won the grand prize at this year's Cannes Film Festival. With a screenplay by Harold Pinter and a cast that includes Julie Christie, Alan Bates, Margaret Leighton and Michael Redgrave it would indeed be difficult to go wrong. Losey's work has never quite gotten the reception that it deserves in this country, but that should all be remedied now. For *The Go-Between* is visually extraordinary and very stirring. (The following paragraph commended the director's technique; one paragraph dealt with story and cast.)

Summary: Vincent Canby's review stands out because he strove to *show*, through the structure and the style of his piece, what the other writers merely *tell* us in a sentence or two somewhere in their reviews. Most of the reviewers (including several not excerpted here) mentioned the Cannes prize and the Losey-Pinter team in the lead, apparently leaning on the traditional journalistic concepts of the "news peg" and "interest in celebrities." Many of the writers cluttered their paragraphs about the story with parenthetical mentions of the actors, a common practice and not usually too intrusive. But Canby's uncluttered, careful paragraphs of story summary manage to capture the "feel" of the picture and to support his conclusions about the strange world in which the characters move.

Catch-22: FIDELITY TO SOURCE

When the film distributors advertised "How did they ever make a film out of *Lolita?*" they did it to titillate the audience, reminding them of the book's erotic nature and arousing their hopes that the film would include more of the same.

When the reviews of the novel *Catch-22* began to appear, the distributors might well have begun to question the wisdom of trying to make a movie out of the best-selling classic of the 1960s. Critical attention (and word-of-mouth communication among filmgoers) centered almost entirely on the perils of adaptation. Almost everyone was disappointed. Some critics were extremely harsh, especially those who were not kindly disposed toward "trendy" director Mike Nichols.

The film's reputation grew constantly during filming, with dozens of Hollywood stars coming to and going from the set and major magazines devoting color spreads and thousands of words of copy to on-location antics and interviews with Nichols. Fans and critics who were wary of possible "tampering" with their favorite book had plenty of time to prepare for not liking the film.

Time magazine scooped the critics by two weeks with a cover article on the film and Nichols. The piece was quite favorable, especially considering *Time*'s ability to humiliate with inference, innuendo and well-chosen anecdote. Perhaps anticipating the attacks on the adapters, the *Time* piece quoted novelist Joseph Heller: "When I saw the film I expected to be disappointed—after all, I had no part of it. But I saw what Mike had done. He didn't try to make it just an antiwar movie or an insane comedy. He caught its essence. He understood." The editors reiterated: "Nichols was not making *Super-M*A*S*H**. From the beginning, he was aware that laughter in *Catch-22* was, in the Freudian sense, a cry for help. It is the book's cold rage that he has nurtured. In the jokes that matter, the film is hard as a diamond, cold to the touch and brilliant to the eye."

Time had the jump on the rest of the critical field, and the producers must have felt relieved. But a few weeks later the other magazines began to weigh in. *Newsweek* discussed the difficulty of transferring the novelist's story to the screen:

In all fairness to Nichols and his screenwriter, Buck Henry, the book had defied all would-be adapters for years. . . . How do you reproduce Yossarian's hallucinatory glimpses of his fellow fighting men, retain their wildly comic calm, their unflappable plausibility, and still make it clear that they, rather than Yossarian, are the nut cases? I don't think Henry ever found a dependable structural answer to such questions, or Nichols a dependable structural stylistic answer, though the movie sometimes comes close to great solutions and sometimes gives the impression of coherence without knowing where its next effect comes from. . . . Heller's novel was too long, Nichols's movie is either too short or too careless with the time it does take. You get the impression that they shot every word of the book (there are no breaks of faith with the text, only with the texture) and then, in desperation, made a final print out of representative snippets.

Three other magazine critics lamented the absence of cohesion, style and mood, and cited the problems created by necessary condensation:

(Hollis Alpert, *Saturday Review*) Joseph Heller's novel, while often belaboring its assumption (with which I am inclined to agree) that military bureaucracy is by its very nature insane, was a wild, exuberant mixture of gruesome realism and outrageous comedy. Somehow it worked, held together by its style. That style hasn't been totally transferred to film. What we have instead is an uneasy blending of two mediums, the novelistic and the cinematic. . . . Heller's people were improbable at times, but they were always people. We got to know them. In the film, they are seldom more than faces. They pass by like figures in a nightmare landscape. . . . Perhaps it was the need to compress so much into a limited time span that caused Nichols to slough off his people, that caused him to choose a form of nightmare—Yossarian's nightmare—in which other nightmares cyclically occur.

(Judith Crist, *New York*) [The film] should be seen because it will, I think, make you turn—or return—to the book to appreciate fully its accomplishment and the difficult task that confronted its screen adapters. . . . I suspect that devotees of the book will find themselves short-changed, but of course nothing less than a 12-hour film could capture the variety that Heller offered, most often on purely verbal terms.

(Lewis Segal, *Show*) All right so no one who loved Joseph Heller's book is likely to tolerate the film of *Catch-22*—there are simply too many favorite characters left out and too many truncated plotlines. But had the film captured Heller's sense of madness instead of settling for a fey and listless eccentricity, it might have justified both the expense and interest which purchase of the book initiated. . . . Buck Henry has attempted to cram a representative portion of Heller's novel into a two-hour mass-audience motion picture. In the process, he has flipped the narrative around so that most of the action is a flashback and has so simplified a number of relationships that the result resembles a series of nightclub sketches placed end-to-end. Henry also has retreated from some of the grimmer implications of his source, satirizing corrupt *individuals* (principally Cathcart and Korn) instead of the insane system Heller attacked. . . . While Heller's characters were simultaneously funny, frightening, and recognizably human, at best Nichols' equivalents aim at these qualities *alternately*, leading to the prevalent stylistic confusion and forced directional diversions.

The most devastating attack on the film came from Stanley Kauffman in *The New Republic.* "There are suggestions that Nichols felt trapped; there is a scent of panic," he wrote of the directing. "He seems to have realized too late the enormous difficulties of filming this book, of conveying its cosmos within a reasonable length, of making *visible* its understated lunacies, of dealing with its changed position in our culture." (The "changed position in our culture"—the growth of the audience's awareness in the nine years between book and film—was also touched upon by most of the film's other detractors.)

Kauffman was one of the few writers who expressed serious reservations about the casting of Alan Arkin in the lead Yossarian role. Specifically, Kauffman scored him for technical limitations in failing to react plausibly to the death of Nately and to the discovery of the mortal wound in Snowden. "The very same film shot for shot would have been immensely improved with a good Yossarian," Kauffman wrote. "Heller's hero is the son of Schweik, emigrated to America and immensely wised up. Arkin's Yossarian is not a resolutely sane man who, by his sanity, seems mad; he is a Jewish-intellectual cabaret comic wallowing in antiheroism as he plays for predictable coterie responses."

Kauffman was most specific in indicating *how* the film might have succeeded:

The book could have been filmed effectively if it had been treated competently as what it is, without nervousness, if its tone had been caught. For me, that tone is neither savage Swiftian satire nor Manichean black humor but the cool extension of the horror and the ridiculousness that are already present in the world: as in Kafka. (Kafka thought his novels were funny.) But the film consistently bumbles that tone—or any other tone. In the book, when U. S. planes bomb their own base as a service to the Germans, so that in return the Germans will buy the Egyptian cotton which Minderbinder's syndicate has overstocked, it is a tart, peripheral, insane note; in the film it is an air raid, with real explosions and real flames. When Yossarian walks desolate through the nighttime streets of Rome, Heller makes it a floating expressionist experience. Here it is a solitary parade past a lot of arbitrary symbols—with Donizetti on the soundtrack. In the book, when the parents and brother of a dying soldier come to visit him and Yossarian substitutes for the boy, it is a scene of shadows and bandages. Here it is played in light, no bandages, and the visitors are three comic actors. A moving symbolic moment becomes a failed skit.

While the magazine critics loosed their salvoes, one major newspaper reviewer—Canby of the *Times*—wrote favorably of *Catch-22*, calling it "the best American film I've seen this year." In his weekday review he devoted only a few lines to the adeptness of the transformation:

It's the special achievement of Heller's novel, as well as of Mike Nichols's screen version, that Yossarian's panic emerges as something so important, so reasonable, so moving and so funny. . . . I do have some reservations about the film, the most prominent being that I'm not sure that anyone who has not read the novel will make complete sense out of the movie's narrative line that Nichols and his screenwriter, Buck Henry, have shaped in the form of flashbacks within an extended flashback. Missing, too, are some relevant characters. . . . Nichols and Henry, whose senses of humor coincide with Heller's fondness for things like the manic repetition of words and phrases, have rearranged the novel without intruding on it.

The following Sunday Canby wrote a long column lavishing additional praise on the film. Virtually the entire piece dealt with the issue of book-into-film. Canby explained that he was one of "the last dozen people in the world who had not read the book" when he first saw the film, was therefore confused, but was dazzled by the film. He read the novel before his second viewing, and came away even more impressed. He spoke favorably about some of the same issues that Kauffman attacked: "It is a movie of valid spectacle, as when Milo Minderbinder, the group's hustling mess officer, contracts with the Germans to bomb and strafe his own base." He called the midnight walk through Rome "an almost literal picturization of an extended passage from the book," which opposes Kauffman's view. (But he agreed that that episode was one of few that jarred.) After discussing the problems inherent in transferring a story from printed page to visual medium, Canby delivered a favorable verdict on *Catch-22*:

Having read the novel when I saw the film the second time, I was able not only to make bridges in the continuity that is otherwise unnecessarily obscure, but also able to marvel at how closely Nichols and Buck Henry, his screenwriter, have been able to approximate, on film, the novel's mood of triumphant madness. They've also been able to retain an extraordinary amount of the narrative that details the terrifying plight of Yossarian. . . . Heller's *Catch-22* is a complex novel, but it's complex on a horizontal plane rather than in the perpendicular plane in which Nabokov operates (and makes him unfilmable). It's a novel that says exactly what it means and that is, in spite of its fantasy, a straightforward accumulation of characters and events. . . . Like Heller, both Nichols and Henry are completely at home in comedy (or drama) of illogic, which owes as much to a tradition of radio comedy favored in the 1930s and 1940s ('It Pays to Be Ignorant') and to vaudeville ('Who's on first?') as it does to *Alice in Wonderland*. By shaping their movie as a flashback that keeps constantly turning back on itself, Nichols and Henry have also found something like the cinematic equivalent to the verbal humor that depends on double negatives of reasoning.
(© 1970 by The New York Times Company. Reprinted by permission)

Summary: Canby was right, the others were wrong. (Start your own argument.)

HEMINGWAY: REST IN PEACE?

When Ernest Hemingway took his life in the summer of 1961, he left more than 300 unpublished works, including complete novels. Nearly a decade later, his wife permitted the release of *Islands in the Stream*, a full-length work, but obviously not polished to the perfection that the author would have desired.

Inevitably, the reviewers addressed themselves to the question of the book's quality and whether or not it was representative of Hemingway. All noted that it was a fictionalization of his own life, and most granted that only parts of the three-section book approached the author's best writing.

The issue upon which there was the greatest divergence of opinion among critics was whether the book should have been published at all. And, since it was published, what lesson was to be drawn from it. A sampling of leading book review sections shows three ranges of opinion, coincidentally paralleling three types of media: Sunday newspapers, where publication was lauded and the worth of the book confirmed; news magazines, which expressed a melancholy ambivalence; and the intellectual periodicals, which added sad postscripts to "Papa's" epitaph.

Asserting that the book was neither the best nor the worst of Hemingway's novels, Robert Kirsch wrote in the *Los Angeles Times:*

> It is a worthy addition to the Hemingway canon. There is no question that it is autobiographical. But then how much of Hemingway's work was not? His favorite themes are here as well. War and the sea, courage and the meaning of life, love and the complexity of relationships. Hemingway is here at his clearest understanding of his world and himself. One cannot ask much more than this. . . . [The novel is] not to be judged solely in literary terms but rather as a testament of a man who for all his faults, his occasional childishness, his posturings, was one of the best we ever had, and through his art made us a part of his search.

The New York Times Sunday review was written by Robie Macauley, coauthor of *Techniques in Fiction.* He gave the book one of its most complimentary reviews, leaving no doubt that he considered it worth publishing:

> Even though he stowed this book away with the idea of doing a little more tinkering, it is a complete, well-rounded novel, a contender with his very best. It has his characteristic blend of strong-running narrative and reflective memento mori and it is 100-proof Old Ernest, most of it. . . . One of the delights of reading Hemingway is to watch the familiar done all over again with just as much verve and force as if it had never been done before. . . . How much better than a monument it is to publish, nine years after your death, a book much finer than any young contenders can write.

Admitting that a review of the book calls for special ground rules, Geoffrey Wolff of *Newsweek* labeled it "a very bad novel with a few bright moments. . . . Hemingway's prose is uncharacteristically loose-gaited, as though the author let his attention to it wander." Wolff then raised the question of whether the book should have been published:

> Before one accuses Mary Hemingway and Scribner's of doing Ernest Hemingway's reputation an injustice it is well to recall that many writers (Franz Kafka, for instance) have been so blind to the merits of their own work that they have ordered their survivors to destroy unpublished manuscripts. No one has the right to suppress a major work by a great writer except the great writer, while he lives. Nonetheless, *Islands in the Stream* should be taken for what it is, a curiosity, an unfinished

draft whose circumstances are untidy and ambiguous. . . . We asked for it, and we got it.

Time magazine's Timothy Foote provided a similar blend, first calling the book a bad novel, then allowing reasons why it might as well have been published:

> The decision may be challenged, for *Islands in the Stream* is in many ways a stunningly bad book. At his best, Ernest Hemingway the writer knew that Papa Hemingway the public figure was his own worst literary creation. One suspects he would have eventually got round to slashing *Islands in the Stream* back by a third or a half its present length. Yet for Papa watchers and Hemingway readers the book is welcome enough. Like the recent sale of backlot stage props from old Hollywood films, its publication seems a commendable act of commerce and nostalgic piety. . . . Only faintly disguised as fiction, Thomas Hudson's recollections of his sons, in life and death, is clearly an attempt by the author to weave some sort of protective magic around them. Hemingway was an openly superstitious man. But anyone with children will find that easy to forgive. What father does not secretly believe he can avert tragedy by imagining it in advance, or hope that he can protect his children by holding them steadily, faithfully in mind and heart?

Most of the reviewers discussed the Hemingway legend and the way it was cultivated by the author himself. In *The New Republic*, Jonathan Yardley made that aspect the focal point of his essay, asserting that "writers grow old uneasily, and often gracelessly, in this country." He termed the Papa image "a shield" and suggested Hemingway could not have lived thirty years beyond his writing prime without it to protect him.

> The real interest *Islands in the Stream* holds is as the definitive delineation of the *papier mâché* Hemingway, drawn for us not by Baker or Hotchner or *Life*, but by the image himself . . . though it is amiable enough, *Islands in the Stream* does not offer much of anything except the legend. It provides no new keys to Hemingway's literary importance. Its narrative is competent (at narrative Hemingway was *never* incompetent), and it contains just enough flickering reminders of his wasted genius to make reading it a frustrating and saddening experience.

What Yardley saw as an American literary phenomenon, Irving Howe in *Harper's* likened to the creative failure explored in Fellini's *8½*. Like the protagonist of the film, Hemingway, according to Howe, apparently "could manage, by now, only ill-connected portions of a narrative—at most, separate panels of representation—

and . . . he must therefore fall back on the plea that the chaos of existence provides a rationale for his inability to achieve a unified work of art." After demonstrating that, in his opinion, the book has no commanding idea, Howe offered a most disheartening summarization:

The conclusion seems to me a terrible one: an artist's, a man's, search for moral growth can disable his performance, crippling him with the knowledge of what he doesn't know.

Writing in *Saturday Review,* John W. Aldridge described the author as living out his fantasies in later life, instead of projecting them in his fiction. He suggested that Hemingway could have escaped his fate:

When he went down into the basement of his house that summer morning and selected the weapon that would end his life, Hemingway evidently forgot about art. It is a pity, because if art had saved him in the past, there was still a chance it might save him once again. There was, in fact, an excellent chance. For, in spite of its defects, the best parts of *Islands in the Stream* make clear that he had in his last years enough talent left to serve art successfully.

Summary: The reviewers who read *Islands in the Stream* as a book first, and as a comment on Hemingway's career second, gave the work its most favorable reviews. Those who approached the book as a possible indication of the state of American letters at the midpoint of the 20th century structured their essays around some larger issue than the book itself, and came to far less favorable conclusions.

Most of the reviewers indicated premonition, if not prejudice, against the book; reading it seemed to bear out what they had suspected. (Many of the book review editors called on professors and anthologists who had studied Hemingway assiduously, so this "predisposition" was not analogous to meanness or unfairness.) None of the reviewers suggested that the publication of *Islands in the Stream* in any way diminished Hemingway's career; they all maintained a reverence for his early writings. None suggested that the remainder of his unpublished writings should be kept locked up; the prevailing, although unstated, view is that it will take another generation to assign "Papa" his final resting place in the annals of literature. Nobody could quite bring himself to say, "Hemingway is dead. Long live Hemingway."

15
Also Worthy
of Mention . . .

The chapter title is recognizable, of course, as the cliché a critical writer uses in the downhill side of his essay to indicate that, in addition to the major elements, a number of other loosely related items are worth mentioning.

CRITICISM AS AN EQUAL OPPORTUNITY EMPLOYER

According to a Louis Harris study, the American mass media critic is typically male, in his 40s and Protestant (except in large metropolitan areas, where he is probably Jewish or unaffiliated). Nowhere are the figures borne out more dramatically than on Broadway, where a corps of white, middle-aged men passes judgment on plays aimed at the entire range of theatergoers.

The study showed that one woman, Judith Crist, ranked among the top three most influential critics, however. (Kerr and Barnes of *The New York Times* were the other two.) Women's Lib advocates might not be entirely pleased with the overall picture, but they would have to admit that women are increasingly respected and well represented in the field of criticism.

Ms. Crist, along with Pauline Kael and Renata Adler, have shown that women are the equals of male film critics, and Ada Louise Hux-table was the first winner of the Pulitzer Prize for criticism. One of the book critics most in demand by the leading literary review supplements is Elizabeth Janeway, long an officer and spokesman for the Authors Guild and the Authors League.

Black critics were virtually nonexistent in the mass media at the beginning of the 1970s. A notable exception is Clayton Riley, who besides serving as arts editor of the *Amsterdam News* contributes to magazines and appears frequently in the Arts and Leisure section of *The New York Times* Sunday edition. Riley was an English major in college, worked briefly as an actor with a touring theater, and covered sports. Now he teaches in college and edits play scripts in addition to doing freelance reviewing.

As a black writer in a white world, however, he is often the "man between" two opposing elements. Militant members of the black community attack any black critic who praises black-made films such as *Shaft* and *Sweet Sweetback* which, to their minds, "co-opt" blacks by focusing on ghetto realities that run counter to militant black politics. And white editors tend to assign black writers only to black topics—a play like *The Me Nobody Knows* or a review of recorded poetry by Langston Hughes. Riley has argued that there is no reason why a black critic should not write about white art forms, since "blacks know what it is to be white," even though whites may not know what it is to be black.

Alfred Kazin, writing in *Commentary*, pointed out that some of the best critics through the years have had what he calls a "sense of being outsiders, whether as Southerners or New York intellectuals. The better world they carried in their heads, whether it was the fiction of the old South as a Greek republic or the new Russia as a humane culture, had given a moral design to their studies." By the same reasoning, might not the American Negro, working from his particular moral design, provide some of the most challenging critical writing of the 1970s? It remains to be seen how soon white editors and readers will comfortably agree.

Another equal opportunity complaint might indeed be lodged by writers and readers outside of New York. While drama, dance and art criticism necessarily center on the nation's cultural capital, there is no reason why such mass media as magazines and television should not work to decentralize the criticism of art forms that are available uniformly throughout the country. Think, for example, of the talent reservoir in Chicago: why aren't Mike Royko, Robert Cromie and Studs Terkel household words like their New York-based counterparts? Think, too, of the talent, intellect and wit to be found on the major Midwestern college campuses.

The answer may well lie in public broadcasting, cable television, and innovations in video communication being explored by others than the monolithic networks. The film buff of 1980 may be able to dial a number at his convenience on a multichannel communications console and bring in a recorded review of the latest Dennis Hopper film. He might even be able to designate a selection of critics from around the country, so that after 15 minutes he'd be exposed to insights and opinions that would otherwise require two hours of digging at the public library.

WHEN IS ENOUGH ENOUGH?

Announcing his retirement after more than a decade of reviewing films in Los Angeles, Burt Prelutsky confessed: "All of a sudden I realized that for the last 12 years of my life . . . I had seen an average of three rotten movies a week. During each year I would see 5 to 10 good movies out of 150. I wouldn't mind paying to see that many movies—which I will be able to choose for myself. That's a lot better than suffering through 140 other pictures for free."

Chronicling her short tenure as a film critic in *A Year in the Dark*, Renata Adler lamented the limitations of the form: "The problem is that reviews are read almost completely for opinions, and with movies this can be especially inadequate. Most movies are not very good. Most people know it and like to see them anyway."

John Simon, in his book *Private Screenings*, made the same observation: "A reviewer elicits mostly one of two reactions: 'Good! That's another one I don't have to see!' or 'Great! I like it already.'" Simon added that the true critic, writing for a more discerning audience, "excites the public's curiosity, wonder, suspicion, rage and enthusiasm."

One of the strongest expressions of frustration may be found in *Newsweek* film reviewer David Slavitt's essay on "Critics and Criticism" in *Man and the Movies*. He characterized his job as similar to reviewing a blizzard or a war:

Also Worthy of Mention . . .

The critic is laughably impotent, has no influence either with the film-makers or with film audiences, has no suitable or adequate vocabulary with which to discuss the films for his putative readers, and, perhaps worst of all, has no position on which to stand, from which to formulate a general theory of what he is trying to do or wants to say, and no way of rationalizing his intellectual career. One cannot write about *Cleopatra* and *8½* in the same week, on the same page, without going a little bit schizy. So one makes it up, one fakes it. I suppose the formula is sociology and psychology for the pop films and belle-lettrist aestheticism for the 'serious' films. But it's treacherous.

It is obvious from the remarks made by these four critics that criticism, as a vocation, takes its toll of the mental faculties, just as surely as black lung disease cuts short the career of the coal miner. *The New Yorker* keeps its film critics sane and healthy by alternating six months of rest with six months of work: precisely at midpoint, Penelope Gilliatt steps in to take Pauline Kael's place, no matter if the most highly touted picture of the year is due in town the next week. *New York* magazine gives Judith Crist half the summer off, replacing her with guest columnists. More than once, Stuart Klein of Metromedia has ended his item with a plaintive: "I need a vacation."

Susan Rice, film critic for *Media and Methods*, a magazine aimed at teachers of visual communications, believes nobody should be a critic for more than three years: "After three years they want to do it themselves." One critic who did just that is Penelope Gilliatt; she wrote the screenplay for John Schlesinger's *Sunday, Bloody Sunday* during her semiannual hiatus. (Fortunately, her associate justices gave her a favorable ruling when she returned to the high court.)

For others, shifting from one art form to another is enough to relieve the tedium and present new challenges. John Simon moved from film to drama criticism, occasionally returning to the former medium. Dwight Macdonald found politics worthy of his critical eye once he felt he had reached a point of diminishing returns with film. Clive Barnes is apparently refreshed by moving back and forth between drama and dance.

Whatever the system, it's clear that the critics need their safety valves . . . or early retirement from the rigors of covering an entire art field year in and year out. The only alternative is a snobbish elitism that permits the writer to choose the works he will discuss, and that's not possible in the mass media.

Curbing cultural inflation

As was true of almost everything in our society, the arts enjoyed a bull market in the 1960s—the term Cultural Explosion was frequently applied to the proliferation of new facilities, the outpouring of literature, and the increased interest in films, fine arts, repertory companies and new modes of creative expression.

Where is it all going? The Ford Foundation hopes to have a better idea during the early 1970s when it begins issuing periodic reports on America's nonprofit performing arts. Initially, 100 orchestras, 40 theater companies, 40 opera companies and 30 dance groups have been studied by a team of economists and systems analysts to determine how they function and how they are financed. The expectation is that compilation and publication of the data will help the people who run cultural institutions to do so more effectively. The reports will also provide those in government, business and philanthropy with a better indication of how financial support should be distributed.

Clearly, the emphasis in the 1970s and 1980s must be on the quality, rather than the quantity, of cultural institutions. A New York consulting firm, engaged to study the cultural climate of one large Midwestern city, recommended that plans for a new arts complex be abandoned. It was a blow to local boosters who had hoped to build a first-rate symphony orchestra and to invite better touring attractions, partly out of jealousy over the more bountiful cultural life of the state's two other leading cities. The consultants suggested instead that more benefits would be derived from improving art facilities in city schools and strengthening already existing institutions. They also advised the cultural affairs committee of the local chamber of commerce, which sponsored the study, that facilities should be centered in the heart of the city, where they could thrive and benefit everyone, not just the affluent suburbanites.

The critic, then, must take care to stimulate *improvement* in the arts rather than saturation. The Minneapolis Symphony Orchestra was reconstituted as the Minnesota Symphony, taking a cue from the successful politics of major league sports. The group plays in both of the Twin Cities and elsewhere in the state as part of its regular season. Extensive school programs are also an important part of its work, along with national and international tours and engagements. The new outlook has meant a greater utilization of musical talent, a better financial situation and a crescendoing reputation for the orchestra.

ONE EYE ON THE RATINGS

We have already established that it is part of the critic's job to be aware of the "prior reputation" of any work he judges. With the increasing popularity of various types of "rating" systems, the responsibility can be vexing.

In November 1968, the Motion Picture Association of America—the film industry's "self-discipline" mechanism—adopted a voluntary classification system for rating movies with respect to their acceptability for young people. After some tinkering with the letter codes, adjusting of the age limits, and redefining of material to be forbidden to minors, the Association settled on four categories, G, GP, R and X. Suddenly the critics had an extra responsibility: deciding whether or not the letter rating for a picture was justified. The fact that the public generally accepted the ratings, and that most parents depended on their accuracy, made it virtually mandatory for critics to mention that there was foul language or embarrassing nudity in a GP picture, or conversely that a film rated R was in fact worthwhile viewing for a minor. Ironically, many films about young people have been rated Restricted merely because of language or nudity that would not surprise or offend most youngsters, while gratuitous violence abounds in many "family" pictures—a phenomenon that many critics have decried in their reviews.

While the film-rating system merely attempts to classify motion pictures, most other ratings with which the critic must contend purport to measure popularity and quality. The television ratings tell the critic that the mindless situation comedies he tries to ignore are enjoying the largest audience. The best-seller lists confirm that the highly publicized sex book of little or no literary merit is selling briskly. And Broadway's longest-running Top Ten chart reflects the public's taste for escapist musical comedies.

What's a critic to do? Slit his throat? Give up?

At the very least, he can try to make us understand *why* mediocre fare is most successful. He can address himself to the issues of how an audience is created, how an insulting piece of claptrap is foisted upon the public, how the best-seller, top-ten and big-hit systems are made to work, and what those who care can do about it. He can make us question many of these practices. He can challenge us to raise our personal standards, so that inferior fare will be left begging while superior fare finds an audience.

Ratings and listings need not be the bane of the critic's existence. They can be a starting point for comparison: "So this is what is alleged to interest or please the typical American at this moment. . . . Let us ask ourselves why." Perhaps some day clever critics will wean us from our Top Ten mentality. In the meantime, they are forced to acknowledge its perverse, pervasive existence.

All the world's a stage . . .

. . . And all the men and women merely players. The neat compartmentalization of criticism—the assigning of each major art form to the appropriate writer—means that the film star, the ballerina and the playwright receive adequate coverage in the mass media. But our cultural milieu is made up of more than just the recognized art forms and the celebrated stars. It includes not only our cultural institutions but our manners and morals as well.

And so, in addition to reviews and criticism of literature, fine arts and performances, we need commentary on what has come to be called our "life style."

Social criticism is nowhere as formalized in the mass media as is criticism of the arts. A few magazines offer political "critics" (as opposed to "columnists") who take an institutional (as opposed to issue- or personality-oriented) view of developments in the political arena. One or two contributors to periodicals such as *Saturday Review* are, in effect, critics of modern English language usage—poet John Ciardi, for example.

But "social criticism" is rarely labeled and displayed as such. It is to be found in the columns of "humorists" such as Art Buchwald and Russell Baker, in the short television vignettes of Charles Kuralt on CBS or Andy Rooney on NET, in the devastatingly cynical or grotesque photo spreads devised by the editors of *Esquire* and *New York* magazines. At its best, it is a five-minute, mini-documentary sequence in *The Great American Dream Machine*—a day in the life of a welfare worker, a visit to the MacDonald chain's Hamburger University, a montage of Sunday in the park, an essay on small town parades, an evening at Roseland Dance City, a sweat-and-groan session at a $50-a-visit reducing salon.

We need to have a better understanding of who we are. To a certain extent it is reflected in our arts, our higher culture, our visible accouterments. But it is also found inside us, and it comes out in our humble utterings, our mundane comings and goings, our reactions to the events that buffet us about from day to day. The best writers and filmmakers have an eye and an ear for what moves us, what motivates us, what hurts us and what makes us happy—all the things that make us what we are. They need more outlets for serving up their slices of life. The most intelligent and imaginative editors understand that some of their space should always be available for pieces which examine the warp and woof of our social fabric—pieces which may not have the immediate impact of the traditional "hard news" items, but which may have even more important long-range effects.

THE THREAT OF A LIBEL SUIT

When criticism is pushed to the limit—when it borders on defamation of character—there is always the threat of a libel suit. The critical writer would do well to understand the basics of libel law rather than depend entirely on his editors to protect him.

The first thing a writer must realize is that customs and mores differ from place to place. Words and phrases that are used without question in the reviews of big-city critics may be construed by a jury of citizens in a small Midwestern city to be defamatory and injurious to the person criticized. Since a writer is judged by his peers, he must be sensitive to the attitudes of his peers—that is, to the community for which he writes. The fact that a similarly scathing attack on an artist performing the same work was published with impunity by *The Village Voice* may not provide adequate defense in a suit brought against the critic writing for, say, the *Charleston News & Courier*.

A landmark 1964 Supreme Court case greatly widened the limits imposed on writers to legitimately criticize "public figures," which is interpreted to include performers and artists as well as public officials. The reasoning behind the decision is basically this: the public figure—by seeking office, or by seeking a mass audience—gives up a great deal of his right to privacy. It is, in effect, more difficult to damage or defame him because citizens have a legitimate interest in his conduct.

The third edition of Paul Ashley's useful handbook *Say It Safely* states: "Once established as proper, criticism may be powerful. Subject to the rules already discussed, the critic can write a philippic. He may condemn in no uncertain terms. He may use satire and proper invective, flanked by a cartoon." The rules included newsworthiness, criticizing in good faith "for the public good," and avoiding discussions of personal life unless they are clearly germane to the public affairs at issue.

Differentiating between the personal life and the public life of an artist may give the aggressive critic trouble. The fact that a ballerina gorges herself on caviar at The Russian Tearoom may have bearing on her performance—she may become pudgy and unsuited for a role as a result. To imply that her appetite is caused by anxiety over her love life, however, clearly pushes beyond the realm of criticism into the perilous area of gossip and slander. *Say It Safely* points out that, while a book may be called shallow and dull, "the review will not be protected as a fair criticism if the author is accused of plagiarism; that charge must be proved true."

A critic is of course not protected if he indulges in falsehoods, abuses of the truth, or malice. Recent liberal interpretations of libel laws do not give *carte blanche* to the reviewer to write whatever he feels like saying.

Selected Bibliography

General

Eliot, T. S. *To Criticize the Critic*, Farrar, Straus & Giroux, New York, 1965.

Fischer, John. *The Stupidity Problem*, Harper & Row, New York, 1964.

Gardner, Helen. *The Business of Criticism*, Oxford University Press, New York, 1969.

Greene, Theodore Meyer. *The Arts and the Art of Criticism*, Princeton University Press, Princeton, 1966.

Hall, Stuart and Paddy Whannel. *The Popular Arts*, Random House, New York, 1964.

Levin, Ira. *Critic's Choice*, Random House, New York, 1961.

Seldes, Gilbert. *The Great Audience*, Viking Press, New York, 1951.

———. *The Public Arts*, Simon & Schuster, New York, 1956.

———. *The Seven Lively Arts*, Sagamore Press, New York, 1957.

Sontag, Susan. *Against Interpretation and Other Essays*, Farrar, Straus & Giroux, New York, 1966.

———. *Styles of Radical Will*, Farrar, Straus & Giroux, New York, 1969.

Tynan, Kenneth. *Tynan Right and Left: Plays, Films, People, Places and Events*, Atheneum, New York, 1967.

Painting, Sculpture, Architecture

Ballo, Guido. *The Critical Eye: A New Approach to Art Appreciation*, trans. R. H. Boothroyd, Putnam, New York, 1969.

Canaday, John Edwin. *Culture Gulch: Notes on Art and Its Public in the 1960s*, Farrar, Straus & Giroux, New York, 1969.

———. *Embattled Critic: Views on Modern Art*, Farrar, Straus & Giroux, New York, 1962.

———. *Keys to Art*, Tudor Publishing Co., New York, 1963.

———. *Mainstreams of Modern Art*, Simon & Schuster, New York, 1959.

Greene, William Chace. *The Choices of Criticism*, M.I.T. Press, Cambridge, Mass., 1965.

Grosser, Maurice Richard. *Critic's Eye*, Bobbs-Merrill, Indianapolis, 1962.

Hook, Sidney. *Art and Philosophy: A Symposium*, New York University Press, New York, 1966.

Huxtable, Ada Louise. *Classic New York: Georgian Gentility to Greek Elegance*, Anchor Books, Garden City, 1964.

————. *Will They Ever Finish Bruckner Boulevard?*, Macmillan, New York, 1970.

Kimball, Sidney Fiske and Lionello Venturi. *Great Paintings in America,* Coward-McCann, New York, 1948.

Kozloff, Max. *Renderings: Critical Essays on a Century of Modern Art,* Simon & Schuster, New York, 1968.

Kuh, Katherine. *The Open Eye: In Pursuit of Art,* Harper & Row, New York, 1970.

Shaw, Theodore, L. *Precious Rubbish, as Raked Out of Current Criticism and Commented On,* Stuart Art Gallery, Boston, 1956.

————. *War on Critics,* Stuart Art Gallery, Boston, 1952.

Stolnitz, Jerome. *Aesthetics and Philosophy of Art Criticism: A Critical Introduction,* Houghton Mifflin, Boston, 1960.

Books, Literary

Brown, Francis, ed. *Opinions and Perspectives from the New York Times Book Review,* Houghton Mifflin, Boston, 1964.

————. *Page 2: the Best of "Speaking of Books" from the New York Times Book Review,* Holt, Rinehart & Winston, New York, 1969.

Cowley, Malcolm, ed. *Writers at Work,* Viking Press, New York, 1959.

Darling, Richard. *The Rise of Children's Book Reviewing in America, 1865–1881,* Bowker, New York, 1968.

DeMille, George E. *Literary Criticism in America: A Preliminary Survey,* Russell & Russell, New York, 1967.

Downs, Robert Bingham. *Books That Changed America,* Macmillan, New York, 1970.

————. *Books That Changed the World,* American Library Association, Chicago, 1956.

Drewry, John E. *Book Reviewing,* The Writer, Boston, 1945.

Hicks, Granville. *Literary Horizons: A Quarter Century of American Fiction,* New York University Press, New York, 1970.

Highet, Gilbert. *People, Places and Books,* Oxford University Press, New York, 1953.

Larrabee, Eric, ed. *American Panorama: essays by fifteen American critics on 350 books past and present which portray the U. S. A. in its many aspects,* New York University Press, New York, 1957.

Latham, Harold S. *My Life in Publishing,* E. P. Dutton, New York, 1965.

Lawrence, David Herbert. *Selected Literary Criticism,* ed. Anthony Beal, Viking Press, New York, 1966.

Lowenthal, Leo. *Literature, Popular Culture, and Society,* Prentice-Hall, Englewood Cliffs, N. J., 1961.

Mansfield, Katherine. *Novels and Novelists,* ed. J. Middleton Murry, Beacon Press, Boston, 1959.

Miller, Henry. *Books in My Life,* New Directions, New York, 1969.

Mitgang, Herbert. *Working for the Reader: A Chronicle of Culture, Litera-*

ture, War, and Politics in Books from the 1950s to the present, Horizon Press, New York, 1970.

Mumby, Frank. *Publishing and Bookselling,* Jonathan Cape, London, 1956.

Oppenheimer, Evelyn. *Book Reviewing for an Audience,* Chilton, Philadelphia, 1962.

Smith, Roger H., ed. *The American Reading Public,* Bowker, New York, 1963.

Van Nostrand, Albert. *The Denatured Novel,* Bobbs-Merrill, Indianapolis, 1960.

Wallace, Irving. *The Writing of One Novel,* Simon & Schuster, New York, 1968.

West, Anthony. *Principles and Persuasions: the Literary Essays of Anthony West,* Harcourt, Brace, New York, 1957.

Dance

Buckle, Richard. *The Adventures of a Ballet Critic,* Cresset Press, London, 1953.

Denby, Edwin. *Dancers, Buildings and People in the Streets,* Horizon Press, New York, 1965.

———. *Looking at the Dance,* Horizon Press, New York, 1968.

Johnston, Jill. *Marmalade Me,* E. P. Dutton, New York, 1971.

Sorrell, Walter, ed. *The Dance Has Many Faces,* Columbia University Press, New York, 1966.

Swinson, Cyril, ed. *Dancers and Critics,* A. & C. Black, London, 1950.

Terry, Walter. *Ballet: A New Guide to the Liveliest Art,* Dell, New York, 1959.

———. *The Ballet Companion: A Popular Guide for the Ballet-Goer,* Dodd, Mead & Co., New York, 1968.

——— and Paul Himmel. *Ballet in Action,* Putnam, New York, 1954.

———. *The Dance in America,* Harper & Row, New York, 1956.

———. *On Pointe! The Story of Dancing and Dancers on Toe,* Dodd, Mead & Co., New York, 1962.

Film

Adler, Renata. *A Year in the Dark: Journal of a Film Critic, 1968–69,* Random House, New York, 1969.

Bazin, Andre. *What Is Cinema?,* University of California Press, Berkeley, 1967.

Crist, Judith. *The Private Eye, the Cowboy and the Very Naked Girl: Movies from Cleo to Clyde,* Holt, Rinehart & Winston, New York, 1968.

Farber, Manny. *Negative Space: Manny Farber on the Movies,* Praeger, New York, 1971.

Fischer, Edward. *The Screen Arts,* Sheed & Ward, New York, 1960.

Kael, Pauline. *Going Steady,* Atlantic Monthly Press (Little, Brown and Co.), Boston, 1970.

———. *I Lost It at the Movies,* Little, Brown and Co., Boston, 1965.

————. *Kiss Kiss Bang Bang*, Little, Brown and Co., Boston, 1968.

Kauffman Stanley. *Figures of Light: Film Criticism and Comment*, Harper & Row, New York, 1971.

————. *A World on Film: Criticism and Comment*, Harper & Row, New York, 1966.

Lindsay, Vachel. *The Art of the Moving Picture*, Liveright, New York, 1970.

Macdonald, Dwight. *On Movies*, Prentice-Hall, Englewood Cliffs, N. J., 1969.

Pechter, William. *Twenty-Four Times a Second: Films and Film Makers*, Harper & Row, New York, 1971.

Reed, Rex. *Big Screen, Little Screen*, Macmillan, New York, 1971.

Robinson, W. R., ed. *Man and the Movies*, Louisiana State University Press, Baton Rouge, 1967.

Sarris, Andrew. *Confessions of a Cultist: On the Cinema 1955/1969*, Simon & Schuster, New York, 1970.

Schickel, Richard. *The Disney Version: The Life, Times, Art and Commerce of Walt Disney*, Simon & Schuster, New York, 1968.

Simon, John. *Movies into Film: Film Criticism, 1967–1970*, Dial Press, New York, 1971.

————. *Private Screenings: Views of the Cinema of the Sixties*, Macmillan, New York, 1969.

Sitney, P. Adams. *Film Culture Reader*, Praeger, New York, 1970.

Tyler, Parker. *Underground Film: A Critical History*, Grove Press, New York, 1969.

Music

Calvocoressi, Michel D. *The Principles and Methods of Musical Criticism*, Oxford University Press, London, 1931.

Demuth, Norman. *An Anthology of Musical Criticism*, Eyre, London, 1948.

French, Richard F., ed. *Music and Criticism: a Symposium*, Harvard University Press, Cambridge, Mass., 1948.

Graf, Max. *Composer and Critic: Two Hundred Years of Musical Criticism*, Norton, New York, 1946.

Kolodin, Irving. *The Composer as Listener: A Guide to Music*, Collier Books, New York, 1962.

Lang, Paul Henry. *Critic at the Opera*, Norton, New York, 1971.

Myers, Rollo, ed. *Twentieth Century Music*, Orion Press, New York, 1968.

The New York Times Guide to Listening Pleasure, Macmillan, New York, 1968.

Pleasants, Henry. *Serious Music—and All That Jazz!*, Simon & Schuster, New York, 1969.

Rich, Alan. *Music: Mirror of the Arts*, Praeger, New York, 1969.

Sherwood, William. *An Essay on Musical Criticism*, Musicana Press, Pomona, Calif., 1954.

Slonimsky, Nicolas. *Lexicon of Musical Invective: Critical Assaults on Composers Since Beethoven's Time*, Coleman-Ross, New York, 1965.

Stasov, Vladimir. *Selected Essays on Music,* Praeger, New York, 1968.
Thompson, Oscar. *Practical Musical Criticism,* Witmark, New York, 1934.

Television

Arlen, Michael J. *The Living Room War,* Viking Press, New York, 1969.
Brown, Les. *Television,* Harcourt, Brace, Jovanovich, New York, 1971.
Carnegie Commission on Educational Television. *Public Television: a Program for Action,* Bantam Books, New York, 1967.
Cole, Barry G., ed. *Television,* Macmillan, New York, 1970.
Coons, John E., ed. *Conference on Freedom and Responsibility in Broadcasting,* Northwestern University Press, Evanston, Ill., 1961.
Ellison, Harlan. *The Glass Teat,* Ace Books, New York, 1970.
Friendly, Fred W. *Due to Circumstances Beyond Our Control,* Random House, New York, 1967.
Glick, Ira Oscar, and Sidney Levy. *Living with Television,* Aldine Publishing Co., Chicago, 1962.
Hazard, Patrick D. *TV as Art,* National Council of Teachers of English, Urbana, Ill., 1966.
Johnson, Nicholas. *How to Talk Back to Your Television Set,* Little, Brown and Co., Boston, 1970.
Miller, Merle. *Only You, Dick Daring!,* Sloane, New York, 1964.
Montgomery, Robert. *Open Letter From a Television Viewer,* J. H. Heineman, New York, 1968.
Schramm, Wilbur. *Television in the Lives of Our Children,* Stanford University Press, Stanford, Calif., 1961.
Skornia, Harry Jay. *Television and Society: An Inquest and Agenda for Improvement,* McGraw-Hill, New York, 1965.
———. *Television and the News: A Critical Appraisal,* Pacific Books, Palo Alto, Calif., 1968.
Steiner, Gary Albert. *The People Look at Television: A Study of Audience Attitudes,* Knopf, New York, 1963.
Texas-Stanford Seminar on the Meaning of Commercial Television, University of Texas Press, Austin, 1967.
White, David Manning, and Richard Averson, eds. *Sight, Sound, and Society: Motion Pictures and Television in America,* Beacon Press, Boston, 1968.

Theater

Altshuler, Thelma C., and Richard P. Janaro. *Responses to Drama: an Introduction to Plays and Movies,* Houghton Mifflin, Boston, 1967.
Braun, Edward. *Meyerhold on Theatre,* Hill & Wang, New York, 1969.
Brustein, Robert. *Seasons of Discontent: Dramatic Opinions, 1959–1965,* Simon & Schuster, New York, 1967.
———. *The Theatre of Revolt,* Little, Brown and Co., Boston, 1964.
———. *The Third Theatre,* Simon & Schuster, New York, 1970.
Esslin, Martin. *Reflections: Essays on Modern Theatre,* Doubleday, Garden City, 1969.

Goldman, William. *The Season,* Harcourt, Brace, Jovanovich, New York, 1969.

Gottfried, Martin. *Opening Nights,* Putnam, New York, 1969.

Hobson, Harold. *Verdict at Midnight: Sixty Years of Dramatic Criticism,* Longmans, London, 1952.

Kernan, Alvin, B., ed. *The Modern American Theatre: A Collection of Critical Essays,* Prentice-Hall, Englewood Cliffs, N. J., 1967.

Kerr, Walter. *Pieces at Eight,* Simon & Schuster, New York, 1957.

———. *The Theatre in Spite of Itself,* Simon & Schuster, New York, 1963.

———. *Thirty Plays Hath November,* Simon & Schuster, New York, 1968.

Lewis, Emory. *Stages: The Fifty-Year Childhood of the American Theater,* Prentice-Hall, Englewood Cliffs, N. J., 1969.

Little, Stuart, and Arthur Cantor. *The Playmakers,* Norton, New York, 1971.

Rowe, Kenneth Thorpe. *A Theater in Your Head,* Funk & Wagnalls, New York, 1960.

"Vintage Critics"

Samuel Clemens ("Mark Twain")

Clemens, Samuel. *Editorial Wild Oats,* Harper, New York, 1905.

———. *The Letters of Quintus Curtius Snodgrass,* Southern Methodist University Press, Dallas, Texas, 1946.

———. *Mark Twain of the Enterprise: Newspaper Articles and Other Documents, 1862–64,* University of California Press, Berkeley, 1957.

———. *Mark Twain's San Francisco,* McGraw-Hill, New York, 1963.

H. L. Mencken

Mencken, H. L. *The Artist: A Drama Without Words,* J. W. Luce and Co., Boston, 1912.

———. *The Bathtub Hoax, and Other Blasts and Bravos from the Chicago Tribune,* Knopf, New York, 1958.

———. *A Book of Prefaces,* Knopf, New York, 1918.

———. *Criticism in America, Its Functions and Status,* Harcourt, Brace, New York, 1924.

———. *Damn! A Book of Calumny,* P. Goodman Co., New York, 1918.

———. *Lo, the Poor Bookseller,* Lakeside Press, Chicago, 1930.

———. *A Mencken Chrestomathy,* Knopf, New York, 1956.

———. *Mencken's Smart Set Criticism,* Cornell University Press, Ithaca, N. Y., 1968.

———. *Newspaper Days, 1899–1906,* Knopf, New York, 1941.

Notte, William Henry. *The Literary Criticism of H. L. Mencken,* University of Illinois Press, Urbana, 1959.

Rascoe, Burton. *H. L. Mencken Fanfare,* Knopf, New York, 1920.

George Jean Nathan

Frick, Constance. *The Dramatic Criticism of George Jean Nathan,* Cornell University Press, Ithaca, N. Y., 1943.

Goldberg, Isaac. *The Theatre of George Jean Nathan,* Simon & Schuster, New York, 1926.

Nathan, George Jean. *The Magic Mirror: Selected Writings on the Theatre,* Knopf, New York, 1960.

————. *Materia Critica,* Knopf, New York, 1924.

————. *Passing Judgments,* Knopf, New York, 1935.

————. *The Popular Theatre,* Knopf, New York, 1918.

————. *The Theatre in the Fifties,* Knopf, New York, 1953.

————. *The Theatre, The Drama, The Girls,* Knopf, New York, 1921.

————. *The World of George Jean Nathan,* Knopf, New York, 1952.

Edgar Allan Poe

Cooke, John E. *Poe as a Literary Critic,* Johns Hopkins Press, Baltimore, 1946.

Evans, May Garrettson. *Music and Edgar Allan Poe,* Johns Hopkins Press, Baltimore, 1939. [Reissued by Greenwood, Westport, Conn., 1968.]

Moss, Sidney P. *Poe's Literary Battles: The Critic in the Context of His Literary Milieu,* Duke Press, Durham, N. C., 1963.

Parks, Edd Winfield. *Edgar Allan Poe as a Literary Critic,* University of Georgia Press, Athens, 1964.

Poe, Edgar Allan. *Literary Criticism,* Dana Estes and Co., Boston, 1884.

————. *Literary Criticism of Edgar Allen Poe,* University of Nebraska Press, Lincoln, 1965.

Whitman, Sarah Helen. *Edgar Poe and His Critics,* Rudd and Carleton, New York, 1860.

George Bernard Shaw

Huneker, James G., ed. *Dramatic Opinions and Essays,* Brentano, New York, 1916.

Kaufmann, Ralph James, ed. *George Bernard Shaw: A Collection of Critical Essays,* Prentice-Hall, Englewood Cliffs, N. J., 1965.

Mencken, H. L. *George Bernard Shaw: His Plays,* J. W. Luce and Co., Boston, 1905.

Shaw, George Bernard. *Advice to a Young Critic, and Other Letters,* Crown, New York, 1955.

————. *How to Become a Musical Critic,* Hill & Wang, New York, 1961.

————. *Our Theatres in the Nineties,* Constable, London, 1948.

————. *Pen Portraits and Reviews,* Constable, London, 1949.

————. *Platform and Pulpit,* Hill & Wang, New York, 1961.

————. *Plays and Players; Essays on the Theatre,* Oxford University Press, London, 1952.

————. *Plays, Pleasant and Unpleasant,* Constable, London, 1931.

————. *The Quintessence of Ibsenism,* Hill & Wang, New York, 1957.

————. *Shaw on Music,* Doubleday, Garden City, 1955.

————. *Shaw on Theatre,* Hill & Wang, New York, 1958.

————. *Shaw's Dramatic Criticism (1895–98),* Hill & Wang, New York, 1959.

Index

Index

Index